Bo

CW00545155

The Pote

MELANIA TRUMP

The Inside Story

BOJAN POŽAR

MELANIA TRUMP
THE INSIDE STORY

Bojan Požar

The Potential First Lady
MELANIA TRUMP – THE INSIDE STORY
The Unauthorized Biography
From a Slovenian Communist Village to the White House
Revised edition

Co-author of Chapters 2 and 3: **Igor Omerza**
Editing: **Tina Bernik**
Translation: **Josh Rocchio** and **Maša Požar**
Design and layout: **HercogMartini**
Cover photography: **Walter McBride – Profimedia**
Back cover photography: **Shutterstock**

Published by: **Založba Ombo d.o.o., Ljubljana, Slovenia**
For the publisher: **Bojan Požar**

CONTENTS

FOREWORD

This is not a book about Donald Trump, nor is it a book about Melania and Donald Trump; this is a book about Melanija Knavs, the shy and skinny girl from Slovenia, a country most Americans, if they've ever heard of it at all, think is part of Russia. Even if they have heard of it, they have probably never heard of Sevnica, the small town Melanija calls – or at least used to call – home. Nonetheless, this Slovenian, this Sevnica native could, as wife to the, at least on paper, most powerful politician in the world – the President of the United States of America, become First Lady.

Her story is full of coincidences and aligned stars, the product of a web of incredible, even spectacularly fantastic circumstances. Her Slovenian colleagues from her modeling days in the 1990s; girls who spent time with her backstage at fashion events such as the then almost cult-like Fashion Bazaar, now barely remember her due to her professional and social unrecognizability. The mathematical possibilities of an average Slovenian model immigrant becoming the First Lady of the United States and assume her place at 1600 Pennsylvania Avenue, are practically impossible to calculate. But now, as of June 2016, this actually seems like a possibility.

Melanija Knavs – today Melania Trump – comes from an entirely average socialist family from Slovenia, born and raised in the former Yugoslavia during the period it was run by the dictator Josip Broz Tito. Her parents were not part of the Slovenian social elite, though her father Viktor Knavs was a member of the Communist Party. They were not rich, but they were not poor either. When Melania met Donald Trump, Donald made a gift of two jackets to her father Viktor, made to measure by the seamstress Silva Njegač from the medieval Slovenian town of Ptuj, whose name will appear again in our story.

Melanija was never the brightest of students; she did not study at Oxford, the Sorbonne, or Harvard (in fact her lack of education and vocabulary is acutely evident in her – most likely due to this reason – rare appearances on her husband's campaign trail); she was never a supermodel, even less a top athlete, a recognized scientist, or a particularly successful businesswoman. Despite this, today, right before her forty-sixth birthday, she is probably by far the richest Slovenian of all time, though the famous prenuptial agreement between Melania and Donald Trump remains the family's best kept business secret.

Melanija Knavs in fact never really had a true career, but her story reads as if scripted in a Hollywood success story, a true American fairytale.

Mitja Čander, author, poet, and head of the Slovenian publishing house Beletrina, upon reading the first edition of *Melania Trump: The Inside Story* when it was published on Amazon, remarked, *"This is the story of a woman who is reborn; she changes her name, language, homeland, lifestyle, and even her body is different. The only thing that has stayed the same is her ambition. To be someone. To be the First Lady of the World."*

And *"she will be an incredible First Lady,"* Donald Trump said of his wife to a crowd of supporters on 4 April 2016 at a rally in Milwaukee.

We know a great deal about Donald Trump, practically everything there is to know. However, not just Americans, but even Slovenians hardly know anything about Melania.

Donald was born on 16 June 1946 in New York in the middle of a run-down district in Queens. His family is of German and Scottish ancestry. Son of the German emigrant Friedrich Drumpf, who after moving to the States changed his name to Frederick Trump, Donald's father, Frederick Christ "Fred" Trump left his poor immigrant family when he was barely eleven years old and started taking care of himself. By the time Donald was born, his father was already a successful construction entrepreneur. Beside Donald, Fred Trump and his wife Mary Anne MacLeod, a Scottish emigrant, had two other sons, Robert and Fred Jr., as well as two daughters, Maryanne and Elizabeth.

Donald Trump clearly got his knack for negotiating with contractors, money lenders, and buyers from his father Fred. By the time he finished college at the prestigious Wharton in Pennsylvania in 1968, he was already worth $200,000 (in today's equivalent over $1,000,000) in his own deals.

In 2005, after his Florida wedding to Melania, journalists from the newspaper *Finance*, published in Ljubljana, the capital of Slovenia, calculated that in 2003, the capital gains tax Trump would have paid had he lived in Slovenia, would have been more than a billion Slovenian tolars, or more than all the companies on the Slovenian Stock Exchange put together. Donald Trump, whose professional empire reaches from real estate to broadcasts of Miss Universe, Miss USA, and Miss Teen USA, is worth about $10.5 billion, a little less than Slovenia's annual state budget. Last year alone he declared an income of $557 million, of which $50,000 were from his Slovenian wife's cosmetic company. He was also a big TV star for a few seasons on NBC's The Apprentice, and he has written several books, the last being *Crippled America: How to Make America Great Again*. He is considered America's most popular billionaire and is, at the moment, best known for his serious bid for the White House.

Intellectuals don't like him, while the middle class eats him up. He enjoys getting into spats with the roughest, toughest, and, as he himself stated in one of his many interviews, *"generally the worst people on the planet,"* namely those working in New York real estate. These are arguments that Donald mostly wins, even though he has almost gone bankrupt three times.

Despite all the particulars of Trump's life offered to us by the media, surprisingly little is known about Melanija Knavs. Inevitably certain details do emerge, such as a few years ago when we were able to read how much her Dior wedding dress cost, and now, with Trump's candidacy for President, the American public has uncovered a few minor details about the life of Melania Trump, which her husband's PR and political advisors sparingly dose out to the media.

Much of this information is effectively staged, embellished, or even photoshopped. Even the well-known British tabloid the *Daily Mail*, which was among the first to write in a little more detail about Melania Trump and which recently ran an article on her as the potential First Lady, has published a great deal of imprecise information in the process.

Slovenian journalists are partly, or largely, to blame for the fog of secrecy surrounding Melania Trump. The lack of investigative research, a true hallmark of post-communist and transitional Slovenian journalism, comes to an absurd head in the case of Melania and Donald Trump, despite the leftward inclination of the majority of Slovenian journalistic circles. This crowd does not like Trump, the Republican, and like him even less now that there is a possibility of him becoming the 45th President of the United States, which explains why they are also ignoring Melania Trump. Most news and articles they write about Mrs. Trump are either based on or simple summaries of foreign media pieces. Throughout this a perplexed Ines Knauss wonders in her Facebook posts why the Slovenian media is not supporting a Slovenian woman in the battle for the White House. Had the man to make "our" Melania First Lady been a young Democrat, and therefore a slightly different political "son in law," rest assured that the Slovenian media would have adored her. If Slovenians were to vote for the next president of the United States, Donald Trump would lose the election by a landslide. According to the one and only opinion poll regarding the American election, conducted by the national daily newspaper *Delo* in March 2016, Trump fares pretty badly. Even though he is the most famous Slovenian "son in law," as the media in Slovenia like to call him, only 10% of Slovenians would actually vote for him. Hillary Clinton on the other hand would get 42% of votes from Slovenian voters. Bernie Sanders, the second Democratic candidate, came in third, while Republican Ted Cruz came in fourth. On the other hand though, the people of Sevnica believe their town could be endowed with "numerous prizes and gifts," should Donald Trump win and Melania become First Lady.

This specifically characteristic duplicity of Slovenian judgment is quite typical regarding the attitude Slovenians have toward Melania Trump. Even though she has not visited Slovenia in over eleven years, and most Americans do not even know she comes from Slovenia, there have even been suggestions a street in her hometown of Sevnica could be named after her. The problem is whether it should be named Melanija Knavs, Melania Knauss, or Melania Trump. The current mayor of Sevnica, Mr. Srečko Ocvirk, says he is open to the possibility of naming a street after Melania Trump, *"because Melania is the most recognized Slovenian person in the world,"* but adds that *"there haven't been any official demands or initiatives regarding the matter so far."*

Our book, researched and written over a period of six months, is an unauthorized biography of Melanija Knavs. One could call it an independent biography as the term "unauthorized" can sometimes bring up a negative connotation with regards to the authors' attitude towards the person in question. That is not the case at all. The authors simply wished for a bit more freedom to write in an unbiased manner without needing the authorization of Mrs. Trump or her famous spouse. The book is about the life of the richest and in a few months perhaps the most influential Slovenian in the world. It is a story full of interesting details, based on written archival material, which is admittedly somewhat limited, as well as numerous stories from friends, acquaintances, ex-lovers, classmates, teachers, business partners, and other peers, both in Slovenia and abroad, including Vienna, Milan, Paris, London, and New York, all the major cities that have colored Melania's life.

According to American stand-up comic Susie Essman, Melanija Knavs, Melania Knauss, or Melania Trump sees in Donald Trump *"a billion dollars and high cholesterol,"* a joke she tells to raucous laughter. But Melania lives a very special, extremely reserved and withdrawn life. Despite our intensive research, it is impossible to find a single picture of her with a personal friend (her only bridesmaid in her grand wedding was her sister), or where she isn't posing in a studied and premeditated manner. Anything resembling an unofficial picture always bears her trademarked frown, a feature that has been seen more often lately, during her evident supporting role in Donald Trump's electoral campaign. When the fake smile is gone, Melania seems either absent or upset, and she is bad at hiding that she would rather be doing something else.

With Donald Trump running for President, Melania has been put somewhat in the background of her husband's presidential campaign. Neither Americans nor Slovenians know anything about her views on politics (yet), as the only statement she has made is that she is only interested in politics at home. What?!

All that is available is superficial and boring information, such as that after Louisa Adams, the British wife of the 6th US President John Quincy Adams, Melania would be the 2nd foreign-born First Lady. This leaves Slovenians, and especially Americans, wondering whether Melania, as First Lady in Washington, might, when she is with her husband in the White house at the end of a long day, as if in a real-life episode of House of Cards, try to convince him to bomb Syria, ISIS, or something else, out of her own political predispositions.

It is probably not enough for her to say in public that, *"Donald will assemble the right people around him. He's a born politician,"* and how she supports him *"from A to Z,"* a phrase that has been mocked by several American journalists. Or that the secret to making their marriage work is having separate bathrooms, or that they usually watch TV in different rooms. Melania herself says that the life she lives is quite hard, but she still manages to master it because it is fun. And even though Donald Trump's attitude towards women can at times be compared to the that of jihadists, Melania says *"he is quite romantic, but in a different way."* Indeed it seems Donald is quite different than most people in many respects.

The course from Melanija Knavs through Melania Knauss to ultimately Melania Trump is a tale of a young girl from a socialist apartment block in Sevnica, born to parents Viktor and Amalija Knavs, who could never have even dreamed for a second that, forty years later, their daughter would be rubbing elbows with the biggest stars in America, or even that she would grace the cover of the fashion Bible Vogue.

All along, as she transformed herself from the extremely shy and reserved girl into the agile and adaptable partner of the immensely wealthy Donald Trump, Melanija Knavs showed all the typical signs of being Slovenian.

Now a naturalized American citizen, Melania seems, in a very Slovenian way, uncomfortable with her roots in Sevnica. This is very similar to how Slovenian girls from the countryside are when they move to the capital Ljubljana to attend college. At the same time, having mostly found her fame and success abroad, she yearns for popularity in her home country. How else can we explain her attempts to silence Slovenian journalists with lawsuits, while still inviting them to have lunch in Paris and write favorable stories about her? Well, such an invitation was in fact only extended once, in the fall of 1998, just before she officially met Donald Trump.

Donald Trump sells in the media. When American tabloids reported on all the dirty details of Trump's divorce from his first wife Ivana, a journalist from Zagreb stated that Mikhail Gorbachev, the eighth and last leader of the Soviet Union and General Secretary of the Soviet Communist Party, could be the person to change the world, but it is Trump who sells newspapers.

Unfortunately not even the authors of this book have been able to establish why Melania doesn't want to return home to Sevnica, why (according to her oldest friends) she has changed so much, and why, on her rare and brief (former) trips to Slovenia or when in contact with Slovenians in the States, she refuses to speak Slovenian.

Even the story of how and when Melania Knauss and Donald Trump met – officially at the Kit Kat Club in Manhattan – is shrouded in conspiratorial secrecy. Melania used never to go out partying, but on the rare night she did, Trump *"immediately"* fell in love, despite the type of women he would previously have paid attention to always being busty blondes. Furthermore, fashion agents maintain that at such parties *"no one was ever interested in Melania."*

During the preparations for the first edition of this book, we attempted to be very accurate, even boringly detailed at times, after all we are dealing with the potential First Lady of the United States and for such a person every tiny detail matters. At the same time we found in researching our stories that, as Donald Trump's presidential campaign progressed, Melania gradually became harder and harder to access. Sources have been shut down and there is literally a physical barrier isolating the Knavs family in New York.

Bear in mind the fact that, at least so far, the American media has not succeeded or has not been allowed to interview Melania Trump's parents. Slovenian journalists, specifically cameramen for the TV show E+ on Slovenia's Kanal A, last managed to capture Viktor and Amalija Knavs at Ljubljana airport in March of 2006, when they flew to New York to celebrate the birth of their first grandchild Barron William Trump.

It is now much clearer why this is the case. Scandals directly connected to the past of the Knavs family, in particular to Viktor Knavs, are like shadows of the past being silently resurrected on Donald Trump's campaign trail. From the secret half brother of the potential First Lady of United States, and an almost creepy confession of Viktor's former mistress about how he pressured her into having an abortion, to membership of Viktor's in the Slovenian Communist party, initially denied by Donald Trump's campaign; all these matters are now being brought to light. Many probably also came as complete news to Donald Trump, with the Knavs family having kept them well hidden. Melania also refutes all reports of her former Slovenian intimate companions, many of whom have, after the release of the first edition of this book, been more willing to speak to reporters.

This book, the revised edition of *Melania Trump: The Inside Story, from a Slovenian Communist Village to the White House,* ends both chronologically and thematically with the birth of Barron William Trump, to date Melania and Donald Trump's only son. This means that many venues connected with the "American" life of the Knavs, or rather Knauss, family remain unexplored. For example, the complicated relationships within the Trump dynasty, where the "Slovenian colony" under the financial supremacy of Melania Trump and the typical family leadership of Viktor Knavs, tries to attain its position within the family.

Judging from conversations with American journalist colleagues, Ivanka Trump is probably the cleverest of the Trump children. Ivanka, Donald's daughter with his first wife Ivana Trump, is vice president of Trump's business empire and always appears physically much closer to her father than his wife Melania during his campaign rallies. Also left unexplained is the life and role of Ines Knauss, Melania's older sister, who occasionally surprises with an intriguing social media post, and who recently moved from Trump Tower to another Manhattan skyscraper owned by Donald Trump. She is officially single and has previously bragged about how it was she who created the Melania Trump brand. At times it seems, understandably to some degree, that Ines Knauss is simply unable to accept the supporting role she plays in the life of her little sister Melania.

The first edition of *Melania Trump: The Inside Story,* which was branded as *"The most thorough biographical account on the life of Melania Trump"* by The New Yorker magazine, and later the Italian *Vanity Fair* magazine, and which a Trump spokesperson described as a book that is *"dishonest, full of untruths and lies,"* gave American journalists the initiative to begin researching and uncovering the family and pedigree of the potential First Lady.

If on the first Tuesday of November this year Donald Trump is elected President of the United States, and Melania becomes *de facto* First Lady, this will be the beginning of a new American political dynasty, one with deep Slovenian roots.

Last but not least, as Americans like to say, at the end of this foreword I would like to warmly thank Igor Omerza, the co-author of the second and third chapter of this book, as well as our team of investigators in the field, who traveled thousands of miles and scoured through countless sources. I would also like to thank the editor Tina Bernik and the translator Josh Rocchio, an American from Maryland who lives in Ljubljana, both of whom have worked especially hard due to time constraints. And of course to my daughter Maša, who lives in Southern France and has coordinated the work done for the PR of the book in the tough trenches that are the American media and literary scene, usually having to also juggle the big time difference between France and Slovenia on one side, and the United States on the other.

Bojan Požar

Ljubljana, June 2016

Chapter 1

JURE, I WILL NEVER GO TO SEVNICA AGAIN!

After the eleven hour flight from Frankfurt, as the Lufthansa plane began its slow descent toward JFK airport, Jure Zorčič was restless, even a little nervous. The reason was not so much the final game of the NBA playoffs between the New Jersey Jets and the San Antonio Spurs he was going to, but the fact that after more than 10 years he was about to see his old flame Melanija Knavs, now restyled as Melania Knauss – or better Trump – spouse of the oft-discussed American billionaire Donald Trump.

Jure Zorčič has, for many years, been one of the most well-known, interesting, and talked about figures in Slovenian media. He is the son of Ivo Zorčič, the retired director of Ljubljana's basketball team Olimpija who coached the team to success in the 1980s and early 1990s, when Slovenia was still a part of Yugoslavia. As a sports functionary, Ivo Zorčič was the darling of the communist elite, especially the last head of the Communist Party Milan Kučan, who after the country's separation from Yugoslavia and its transition to a parliamentary democracy in 1991 also became the first President of the Republic of Slovenia. As one of its main tools for promoting the regime, the Communist Party had always invested heavily in sports. Of course many prominent, influential sports politicians, among them Ivo Zorčič, struck it rich as a result. Olimpija's sponsor back then was the Slovenian and international construction company Smelt, an organization run by the firm hand of those in Milan Kučan's inner circle, but which suffered a quick and miserable decline during the transition to a market economy.

The Ljubljana-based company Smelt, later renamed Gio, whose last CEO was Ljubljana native Savo Tatalović, appears in Melanija Knavs' career once before, in 1988, when a handful of select Slovenian journalists were invited to a special PR meeting with Melania Knauss; they flew to Paris on a private jet owned by Smelt/Gio.

Zorčič Senior's affinity for sport also rubbed off on his son, Jure. After his father Ivo's death, Jure Zorčič became a sport manager, but very soon went bankrupt. In the aftermath he started a career in sports journalism. He is now no longer a journalist or manager, though, some years ago, he did help build the career of the Slovenian swimming champion and silver medalist at the Beijing Olympics, Sara Isaković, who later became a student and swimmer at the prestigious Berkeley University, but he is still one of the most informed individuals in sports circles, especially when it comes to basketball.

Jure Zorčič is usually dressed in designer clothes and surrounded by famous Slovenian women. Years ago he was one of the Slovenian jet-setters, popular and ever present at countless elite parties, where there was no shortage of drugs and alcohol. His list of lady friends includes former Miss Slovenia Iris Mulej, whose modeling career took her to Milan without real success, the established theater actress Nataša Barbara Gračner, and until recently, PR agent and TV producer Saša Lipej.

Despite the pretty, popular girls and expensive, fancy clothes, Jure Zorčič has always had a problem with money, more accurately with running out of it. He has even been mocked by some as the homeless cosmopolitan. There were times when he was rumored to owe money to half of Ljubljana, something fairly typical of the endless playboys and quasi-entrepreneurs from the early days of Slovenia's transition to capitalism. Today he likes to brag that his financial troubles are a thing of the past. He does a little bit of everything, from selling bio-fuel for the German company Verbio, to a number of other smaller endeavors. There were even stories around Ljubljana about how he did not even have the money for his ticket to New York and was forced to sell one of his Top Gun style leather jackets.

In New York, Jure Zorčič stayed at the historic Mayflower Hotel on 15 Central Park West and 61st Street. It was a 4-star hotel at a practical location for visitors to Manhattan. Soon after he arrived he headed off toward Trump Tower on Fifth Avenue, where the Trumps stay whenever they are in New York. Melania told Zorčič that they split their time between Manhattan and their other homes in Florida's Fort Lauderdale and Virginia.

Melania and Donald Trump's enormous Manhattan penthouse is on the 66th floor of Trump Tower, with its 3 floors overlooking Central Park, decked out in their signature gold. Aspects of this apartment, dazzling in its kitschy gold, were recently put on display to the American and global public, when Melania Trump posed, Miss America style, for the magazine *Harper's Bazaar*.

What a change, Zorčič smiled to himself. When Melania and he were dating, the current serious contender for First Lady of the United States lived with her two years older sister Ines in a rented, then eventually bought, typical two-bedroom socialist-era apartment, with her father Viktor Knavs paying the rent.

Upon arriving at Trump Tower, Zorčič was confronted by a tall, black doorman. Jure tried explaining that he had come from Slovenia and was here to visit Melania. Of course, he never dared mention that they had once dated.

The doorman insisted that Melania Knauss did not live there. Jure Zorčič knew that this was a necessary bluff, that the man was probably under orders, so he tried a different tactic. He found one of his business cards and on the back wrote down his hotel room number at the Mayflower, and handed it to the doorman. It clearly worked, as the doorman took the business card and, as it turns out, gave it to Melania Knauss.

Melania called her former boyfriend Jure at the Mayflower two days later. Once cannot but wonder what she was thinking at that moment, and what she remembered of their relationship. One thing is certain: in the five years since she and Donald had gotten married, this was the first time she was making a phone call to a 4-star hotel.

Jure Zorčič was deeply moved, hearing her voice for the first time after ten years. He later told the story that he was probably the last and only friend of hers from Slovenia who had seen her in person. In a couple of months' time he could also be one of at least five famous Slovenians to have slept with the First Lady of the United States.

He thought about how they had ridden on his Vespa scooter through the streets of Ljubljana. During Slovenia's ten-day long war of independence they had even ridden between the barricades that the police and civil guard had put up in case the Yugoslavian People's Army would decide to attack from the infantry barracks located within the capital. Years later, already during Trump's presidential campaign, Melania embellished a few details for *People* magazine, turning these Vespa rides into her witnessing the fall of Communism.

"I lived through the fall of Communism in Slovenia in the early '90s before studying design at the University of Ljubljana, and launching a career as a model," she said. This is how Trump's election campaign advisors spun it, and it is merely one of many made up, dishonest, or at least somewhat skewed public statements that Melania has given since becoming Mrs. Trump.

In March 2016, when reporters from foreign media outlets began coming to Slovenia, mainly to Ljubljana and Sevnica, to report on Melania Trump, they also met with Jure Zorčič. Now 48, Zorčič, who met Melania for the first time when he was 23, told the team from the American ABC television network all about how he met Melanija Knavs in old town Ljubljana in 1991, while on his scooter,

"I was on my Vespa and she was walking down the street. I drove past her, coming down the hill on Gornji Trg Square, and then began asking myself who this girl was. She was so beautiful, I just had to turn around and go after her." As he gave this detailed report of their meet cute, he gestured to the reporters how he turned the Vespa, making brrr, brrr motorcycle sounds all the time. This bizarre and almost humiliating scene in the video of his account was aired on TV and circled the globe.

Zorčič asked Melania out for a coffee and she initially turned him down before eventually agreeing. According to him, her demeanor was sophisticated and polite; they found out that they had common friends who usually met up in the evenings by the river Ljubljanica, which runs through the center of the Slovenian capital. *"We went for coffee. From the second I met her, I was impressed by her beauty. She was fashionably dressed, in leather shorts with elastic straps, and had an elegant demeanor. She was tall with long hair; I could barely see her eyes."* Today Jure Zorčič says he had never before or since seen a girl dressed as simply, yet as beautifully as her.

After this first meeting, Zorčič and Melania dated for a few months and even went on vacation together to the Croatian seaside resort of Opatija. Zorčič also visited her in their apartment on Glinskova Ploščad 20 in Ljubljana. He also once took her to visit his sister. When his sister asked her what she wanted to drink, the future Mrs. Trump asked for a glass of plain water, which she then sipped calmly and slowly.

Zorčič told the American reporters that, when they dated, Melanija was *"a typical Slovenian girl and no one had the slightest idea that she would once reach the top of the world."*

Ljubljana's Vespas, a scooter brand made by the Italian company Piaggio, seemed to be, as we shall see later, an attractive trait for the young girl from Sevnica, as every single Slovenian lover she was involved with had owned a Vespa. Despite Zorčič's detailed description of how he met Melania which was also published in the *Daily Mail,* Donald Trump's PR spokesperson Hope Hicks denied the story, labeling it fiction. As for Jure Zorčič, who presented himself as a businessman and manager to the foreign reporters, the Daily Mail also wrote that in 2011 he was accused of embezzling 14,000 euros, while working for the Serbian-Slovenian TV network Pink. This was supposed to prove that Zorčič had lied in the past though the *Daily Mail* did also write that it was unclear whether the accusations made about Jure Zorčič by the owner of the Pink TV Željko Mitrović were true. Jure Zorčič said he was perplexed over Trump spokesperson Hope Hicks' denial, Melania was 28 years old when she met Trump, *"What did he think? That she was still a virgin?"*

But Hope Hicks, the 27-year-old former model and lacrosse player, now Trump's head of PR, who rose to this position without any particular political experience, is also a target of much criticism. Forecasts that she will probably regret working as Trump's PR person are as constant, with the anti-Trump camp claiming that Trump's campaign *"is the most fascist campaign in recent history of the United States."* Hicks is the one that controls who gets to interview Donald

Trump, selecting from around 250 daily requests that arrive at the PR department. She is also responsible for many of Trump's most shocking tweets, which are dictated to her by her boss. These tweets have included Trump's attack on Pope Francis and on the American journalist Michelle Fields labeling her as *"a lying, attention-seeking bitch,"* after she accused Corey Lewandowski, the now former head of Trump's election campaign, of physically attacking her during a Trump rally at the National Golf Club in Florida in March 2016. Public relations, however, seem to suit Hicks well and PR is almost a Hicks family tradition. Her father, Paul B. Hicks III, was an executive director of a public relations firm, as well as the executive vice president of communications at the NFL (National Football League). Her deceased grandfather Paul Hicks II was the vice president and general public relations director at Texaco.

For Jure Zorčič his romance with Melanija was beautiful, but she never wanted to commit to a more serious relationship, as she was already being pulled by the fashion world of Italy and France.

Melania suggested that she and Zorčič met at Café SFA, the restaurant at the top of Saks Fifth Avenue flagship store in Manhattan.

Jure Zorčič, curious and above all a little anxious, hurried to Fifth Avenue by taxi. As he sat at the Café, his first visit to the venue, he immediately saw why Melania had suggested this location, the view of Fifth Avenue is simply stunning, an impressive sight for anyone on their first trip to New York. The best part of it is the view of Rockefeller

Center and St. Patrick's Cathedral, which was recently renovated to the tune of $247 million. Many of the cafe's foreign visitors come simply for the view of Manhattan, not to mention that the menu at the top of the famous department store is tailored to the tastes so characteristic of the city. The most popular items are salads and chicken or tuna sandwiches, as well as their minestrone soup. The ambiance is peaceful, and instrumental music is played in the background.

Melania arrived accompanied by a tall, muscular bodyguard, who, dutifully well-trained and considerate, sat down a few yards away. As soon as Zorčič noticed the bodyguard he realized that this meeting, all these years later, would not be remotely like the encounters he had been used to. Clearly Melania, by then already the insanely wealthy Mrs. Trump of five years, never went – or was maybe even not allowed to go – anywhere without guards. Not even, or perhaps especially not, for a friendly chat with a former boyfriend from Slovenia. He understood that this meeting, probably their only one, would be almost formal in nature. They greeted each other with a hug and kissed each other on the cheeks. Americans are more outgoing in their displays of affection, a trend that is slowly and torturously making its way across the pond to Slovenia. With the exception of Slovenians living on the coast, next to the famously affectionate Italians, interpersonal relationships in Slovenia are slightly colder, more withdrawn, and much less open than in America.

Melania sat down and ordered an orange juice. Jure Zorčič observed her closely.

"She appeared very artificial," he later told his friends with a tone of disappointment. He commented that when they dated she *"didn't have a large bosom,"* a fact noticed by many fashion agents, headhunters, models, and photographers, *"but now, all of a sudden... huge boobs, and her finger joints looked ceramic. Even by then it was obvious she had undergone numerous cosmetic surgeries. She was still very beautiful, though."*

The young Melanija's relatively flat chest was something that her first boyfriend and the man she lost her virginity to, Peter Butoln, also remarked on. Peter Butoln also had a relationship with Melania's sister Ines.

What had not changed were her trademark feline eyes, which, when the then 22-year old Melania Knavs hit the catwalk for the first and last time at the Slovenian beauty contest Look of the Year organized by the Slovenian women's magazine Jana, were immediately noticed – and are still remembered to this day – by the Slovenian-Croatian TV producer Petar Radović, who had directed the pageant at the Slovenian coastal resort of Portorož.

Exactly thirteen years later, Petar Radović was the subject of a lawsuit by Donald Trump against *Slovenske Novice*, the most widely-read Slovenian tabloid, with Melanija Knavs, by then Mrs. Trump, professing not to know Petar at all, and, with the article that mentioning Radović and Knauss, Trump's lawyers claiming it *"negatively slandered the good name and reputation of Mrs. Trump."*

More than by her silicone breasts, Zorčič was shocked by the fact that Melania started speaking to him in English. He looked at her in surprise, then insisted that they spoke

Slovenian. Melania gave in and switched back to her native language.

A well-known Slovenian businessman found himself in a similar situation to Jure Zorčič; Janez Škrabec, CEO and co-owner of the logistics and civil engineering company Riko, made a fortune in Russia and knows Vladimir Putin along with several other influential Russian tycoons and politicians personally, and is one of Slovenia's wealthiest entrepreneurs. A few years ago he met Melania Knauss at a reception in Florida. When Škrabec, native of the small Slovenian town of Ribnica, not far from Melania's hometown of Sevnica, approached her and addressed her in Slovenian, Mrs. Trump rudely cut him short, saying, *"English, please!"* The surprised and somewhat disappointed Janez Škrabec, a man known for his politeness and friendliness, had no other choice but to continue in English, only complaining about the matter later to his friends and acquaintances.

When this news made it to Slovenian media, Melania Trump was condemned in a storm of online comments. One angry commentator wrote, among other things, that, *"Melania Trump rarely opens her trap, but there's a clip from the States where she does. And when she does, you can't believe your ears. The woman has been living abroad for 25 years, married an American, and clearly suffers from the Balkan psychological complex, she won't ever speak a word of Slovenian, not even by accident. That's what makes it so weird, even shocking, that she never lost her accent, that thick, Russian-sounding accent. She pronounces the letter L like a Serbian from deep in the Balkans, and everything else like a Russian from some remote village (a village smaller than her native Sevnica, of which she is ashamed). In the video the reporter asks* her a question, she starts babbling like a high-priced escort with a Russian accent. If she hasn't spoken Slovenian in over 20 years and is so ashamed of the language, as well as of the country she was born in, and which gave her a free education, how can she even be the wife of an American presidential candidate? I know a lot of Slovenians around the world, some of them much more famous than she is – especially for their own work – all she did was marry a millionaire, and none of them find it below their pride to speak in their native language if the person they're talking to is from Slovenia. Many of them teach their children their native language, since knowing a language spoken by just 2 million people can only be an added value, not a loss. All I'm saying, Trump would be just fine without the bimbo standing next to him who is ashamed of her own identity, her home... She has that much money and can't even master a proper accent; someone could even work with her every day, so she became a little more socialized... So much spitting on her fellow countrymen, on Slovenia, but you can barely understand her American English. If anyone has ever heard her trying to speak, you know what I'm talking about..."

Perhaps understandably, Slovenians are, mostly due to historical circumstances, known to be particularly sensitive about their language. As claimed by history books, Slovenians, this small central European nation locked between the bigger German, Roman and Finno-Ugric realms, survived mainly because of their language and culture.

Another interesting story regarding Slovenian was disclosed by the fashion designer Maja Ferme. In 2005 Ferme flew to New York to work for GenArt and the designer Anna Sui. At a party she met a woman who lives in Trump Tower. The New Yorker invited her home, and happily told Maja during her visit that there were already two Slovenians living in Trump Tower. She of course meant Melania Trump and her sister Ines. When Ferme told her that she had never met Melania, the woman was surprised and asked her husband to take Maja up to the Trumps. Sure enough, Maja Ferme went with her host to the top of Trump Tower, where the Trumps have their apartment. She was received warmly, and Melania talked with her about design and living in New York – but all in English, not Slovenian. Melania said this was because of Donald, who did not understand Slovenian. It was then Donald who intervened, saying it was time the two switched to their native language. He apparently really enjoyed himself listening to the two speak in Slovenian.

That was August 2005; Melania and Donald also trusted Maja with a secret, namely that Melania was pregnant. This news would only become official in October of the same year.

It appears that Donald Trump generally likes pretty Slavic girls who speak with, what is often called in the west, a Russian accent. His ex-wife, the famous Ivana Trump, née Zelníčková, who was a Czechoslovakian skier and model – though the Czechs say she was only ever a second-string skier – still today speaks English with a thick 'Russian' accent. This is despite the fact that she met Trump in a restaurant right back in 1977, a year after she had traveled to New York as a Canadian immigrant to promote the Olympic Games in Montreal. One thing at least we have to thank Ivana for is thinking up Trump's nickname: The Donald. He is still called that when people are trying to poke fun at him.

In October 2015 Ivana Trump took a jab at Melania Trump as the potential future First Lady. At an elite party in New York, she jokingly, though lucidly and politically, cracked a joke about the current role Melania plays in Donald Trump's campaign, *"What is he going to do with his third wife? She can't talk, she can't give a speech, she doesn't go to events, she doesn't (seem to) want to be involved."*

Jure Zorčič will probably never forget how, during their chat at the Café at Saks, high above New York, Melania swore to him, directly and in English, *"Jure, I will never go to Sevnica again!"*

Zorčič even gave her a suggestion of something she might do for her home country, a profitable suggestion, of course. She could, for example, start a club of Slovenian and American businesspeople. As always, he must have also smelt an opportunity for himself. Nonetheless, he got the impression that Melania was not at all interested in anything like that.

It was only a few months later, in August and September of 2011, that the Trumps, through their brand Trump Home, which sells furniture, lighting, decor, mattresses, and bedding, began promoting a prestigious line of crystal from the famous Slovenian glassworks at Steklarna Rogaška, close by to Melania's hometown of Sevnica. Donald Trump put his personal effort into the promotion and on 14 September, with an air of confidence only he is capable of, stepped into Macy's in New York and signed his name onto products made in Slovenia using a special fine-tip pen. At the event Trump shook hands with the CEO of Rogaška USA, Mr. Boštjan Leskovar, but Melania was nowhere to be found, which is a bit strange given that it was a deal made by both Trumps with a company from Melania's native country, Slovenia. Leskovar appears not to have known why she was not there, and was unable even to tell reporters present whether the Rogaška deal was the result of Melania persuading Donald. He did not, perhaps solely out of politeness, exclude the possibility that Donald and Melania discussed things before signing the deal. Representatives of Rogaška are said to have first reached out to Trump by telephone, and it took three months to iron out the details.

Leskovar was more than satisfied with the deal. He boasted that Steklarna Rogaška would now have an exclusive license for manufacturing the Trump Crystal Gifts brand, making them the sole Trump crystalware producer. They had bought the license, but Boštjan Leskovar was unwilling to disclose how much they had paid for it. Rumor in professional circles has it that Trump made them pay a pretty penny for it. The contract they signed with Donald Trump was for five years, set to expire in August 2016, with the option of extension. The prices of Slovenian products from the Donald Trump Crystal Gifts collection, advertised as being *"made from the finest Rogaška crystal, so people can incorporate the luxury and style of the Trump lifestyle into their homes,"* ranged from 25 to 600 dollars. Advertisements also claimed that the products *"were made not far from the birthplace of Trump's wife with Slovenian roots, Melania Knauss."*

Four years earlier, in January 2007, Steklarna Rogaška became a member of the prestigious New York American Academy of Hospitality Sciences. This was barely a month after they had been saved from bankruptcy by the financial fund Julius. At the time the AAHS had around 250 members, most of them billionaires, who personally vouch for the quality and prestige of recognized products with the Five Star Diamond Award plaque. Steklarna Rogaška was recommended for inclusion in the club by the Croatian Vladimir Kraljević, whom Slovenians know as the Croatian rights-holder to the Miss Universe contest. Kraljević considers himself a personal friend of the Trumps, and takes every opportunity to point this out.

As the owner of the Croatian Miss Universe and CEO of the Croatian agency Media Produkcija, Vladimir Kraljević was involved in a serious and bitter lawsuit in 2012 with one of the Miss Universe contestants, a certain Martina K. The up-and-coming Croatian beauty accused Kraljević of attempted rape. He insisted in court that she was lying, and that she was actually trying to blackmail him, even to kidnap him. He claimed to have been saved from the kidnapping by his lawyer, and his wife Marija Kraljević corroborated his story. Vladimir Kraljević was also friends with Trump's first wife Ivana, as well as his father Fred Trump, who passed away in 1999.

Finance, the only Slovenian business journal, considered Steklarna Rogaška's inclusion in the AAHS as, *"great success for a Slovenian company."* The then General Manager of Steklarna Rogaška, Mr. Robert Ličen, expressed gratitude for *"the friendly relations between our glassworks, Kraljević, and Trump."* Ličen also attributed part of the deal's success to *"Melania Trump's Slovenian roots,"* but the ace in the hole was Steklarna Rogaška's gift to the Trumps of a crystal cradle upon the birth of their son, Barron William Trump.

The glass cradle was designed by Steklarna Rogaška as a creative gift, inspired by Slovenian heritage, etched with the classical pattern of the Slovenian national flower, a mountain carnation, gold-plated, engraved with the name "Barron William Trump" and hand-blown into a metal mold in the traditional way. The glassworks assigned only its most accomplished master blowers to work on the unique gift. It was a painstaking process to attach the glass rockers and the four decorative crystal balls that adorned the top.

Steklarna Rogaška USA were thrilled and honored to send the cradle to Trump's son, and they expected, as custom would dictate, at least a friendly thank you note from "our Melania" and "Slovenia's son-in-law" Donald Trump. But the eagerly awaited letter from New York never arrived. Unlike with Trump, Steklarna Rogaška received a handwritten thank you from former US President Bill Clinton, appreciating the gift they had sent and the token of respect.

Many other well-known personalities around the world have received gifts from Rogaška, including violinists Isaac Stern and Stefan Milenković, ski jumper Martin Schmitt, Russian President Vladimir Putin, another US President George W. Bush, the late Pope John Paul II, Queen Elizabeth II of England, and many more. Rogaška point out that they have received thank you notes from each and every one of them, apart from the Trumps.

Steklarna Rogaška, a traditional Slovenian company with a long history, is no longer in Slovenian hands. First it was taken over by the American company WWRD, and a few months ago by the Finnish Fiskars Corporation. Robert Ličen who was, after the 2008 parliamentary elections in Slovenia and the victory of the Social Democrats, even on Prime Minister Borut Pahor's shortlist for the post of

Finance Minister, was not CEO of Steklarna Rogaška for a long time. He moved on to become Chairman of the Supervisory Board of the national highway company DARS, a post he was actually recently removed by government representatives, or rather Slovenian Sovereign Holding, the company managing state assets of Slovenia. Robert Ličen is today considered to be one of the biggest critics of the current Slovenian Prime Minister Miro Cerar's government.

Donald Trump also found himself directly involved in another business story from Slovenia, this time in connection with the capital, Ljubljana, and its famous tallest building called Nebotičnik (The Skyscraper). About ten years ago, Marko Bricel, a Slovenian businessman from Toronto and son of the well-known Ljubljana construction mogul Ivan Bricelj who built the Nebotičnik in the 1930s, inquired as to whether Trump might be interested in buying the famous building.

"The idea that Donald Trump might buy the Nebotičnik was mine," Marko Bricel, who dropped the silent "J" from his surname after moving abroad to prevent problems with pronunciation, told the media recently. He saw that the building had been seriously neglected due to its owners' financial difficulties. As the son of the director of the Ljubljana-based construction company that had built the Nebotičnik, he was *"sad to see one of Ljubljana's most important buildings in such a miserable state."* He thought that Trump's ownership could "save" the building.

Marko Bricel reached Donald Trump, then already married to Melania, through some of his personal acquaintances, specifically through a family friend, Trieste native Gianna Lahainer-Lombardi, vice-president of Trump Towers. Bricel approached Trump in a professional and intellectual move by sending him a book entitled *Nebotičnik the Skyscraper of Ljubljana: Money and Architecture*, written by Slovenian architectural historian Bogo Zupančič, whom Bricel had also consulted to inquire what the Nebotičnik was worth and who its owners were. Among its important owners, for instance, were the influential pension fund management authority Kapitalska Družba, which had, five years previously, sold the top two floors of the Nebotičnik to the Slovenian Australian Anthony Tomažin. Bricel even invited the historian Zupančič to come with him to New York, to present the project to Trump in person, but the sale fell through before this could happen.

According to Bricel, Trump is reported to have read the English part of the book about the skyscraper with interest. He even sent him a letter, saying he was *"honored"* that Bricel *"presented the project of buying the Nebotičnik, and that he had no doubt the project would be a success."* But the letter also stated that he, *"currently had a number of loose ends to tie up in the States and could not take on another project,"* finally also thanking him for the *"excellent book about the Nebotičnik."*

The well-known Croatian plastic surgeon Siniša Glumičić, who in January 2005, just days before Donald and Melania's much publicized wedding, publicly boasted about having operated on Melania, told the Croatian newspaper *Slobodna Dalmacija* that Melania rarely returns to Slovenia. He used a slightly patronizing tone and was of the opinion that Melania has renounced her homeland Slovenia because hundreds upon hundreds of Slovenians have been bothering her with various business, financial, and other favors, that it is understandable that she has *"changed all her phone numbers and cut all ties to Slovenian media."*

What and when on Melania Knauss Siniša Glumičić is supposed to have cosmetically corrected at his clinic in Zagreb remains unclear. Given how Jure Zorčič spoke about Melania being *"extremely skinny and lacking any notable chest circumference"* and about how she used to wear a B-size bra, we assume that Glumičić must have enhanced them at some later point, likely even after she had met Donald Trump. With Siniša Glumičić considered as the top Croatian plastic surgeon, performing operations for the Balkan jet setting elite and, as a result, also charging a hefty price, we can assume that it was Trump who financed her plastic surgery, or even surgeries. Still cheap by comparison for Trump, this was also logistically extremely practical; When visiting her hometown, Melania could just hop down to Zagreb, less than fifty miles away from Sevnica and avoid the tabloids.

Glumičić says that the procedure was *"corrective,"* even though Melanija was, in his opinion, already beautiful before the operation, the operation made her *"radiant."* Peter Butoln, who kept in contact with the Knavs family until 2012, not via Melania but her sister Ines Knavs, believes Melania had her first plastic surgery even before she met Donald Trump.

Despite his purported connection to Melania, Siniša Glumičić, had willy-nilly to admit to the media that, he was not among the recipients of an invitation to Donald and

Melania's wedding in Palm Beach, at Trump's property Mar-a-Lago. It is likely, in fact probably certain, that the invitation never came because of Siniša Glumičić' tendency to boast in private circles in a less than discreet manner that he and Melania had also been intimate. This must have reached the ear of the bride and groom, but there was also doubt as to whether Glumičić exactly ranked among the global elite that Donald and Melania had invited to their wedding, for example the legendary American Secretary of State Henry Kissinger, British singer Elton John, the famous actress Liza Minnelli, the British heir to the throne Prince Charles, the American TV superstar Oprah Winfrey, the Italian tenor Luciano Pavarotti, the boxing legend Muhammad Ali (when Muhammad Ali died on 4 June 2016, Donald Trump tweeted: *"Muhammad Ali is dead at 74. A truly great champion and a wonderful guy. He will be missed by all!"*), Hollywood star and future California governor Arnold Schwarzenegger, and many others, all beautiful, famous, and rich. Had the Croatian surgeon Siniša Glumičić received an invitation, friends and acquaintances say he would have taken the first plane out to Florida.

Siniša Glumičić is now married to a Slovenian, Metka Hajnc from Radlje ob Dravi, and they have three children. Another unusual story in connection with the couple and the rumors spreading from Metka's hometown, about her father living as a homeless person.

Connected at least three times to Melanija Knavs and Siniša Glumičić is also the story of the well known starlet from Ljubljana, Inja Gregorič, a girl the same age as Melania. She and Melanija posed together as young models for the Jutranjka clothes company from Sevnica. Siniša Glumičić is said to have performed breast-enlargement surgery on both Melanija and Inja, and also purports to have dated both. Melania went on to meet Trump, but the blonde Inja Gregorič, personal escort of numerous famous Slovenians including pop singer Jan Plestenjak and the much older Swiss/Slovenian businessman and Honorary Slovenian Consul in Croatia Božo Dimnik, later got to privately meet the former US president Bill Clinton when he came to Ljubljana in late 2009 as an honorary guest of Diners Club Slovenia.

Slovenian media has often accused Melania Knauss of deliberately forgetting her Slovenian roots. Donald Trump, for example, has never set foot in Melania's hometown of Sevnica, though it is true that Melanija was not actually born in Sevnica but in the town of Novo Mesto not far away. Since their marriage, the Trumps have only once come to Slovenia together, and even then only for a couple hours. After stepping out of their plane at the airport near the capital Ljubljana, they briefly visited the nearby picturesque Lake Bled, and then went straight back to the airport.

Despite all her attempts to cut ties with her homeland and the fact that she has been living in New York for twenty years, Melania cannot seem to lose her typical, Slavic accent when she speaks English. Her son Barron also speaks English with a Slavic, or specifically Slovenian accent, and is also said to speak Slovenian and French. Melania and Barron's Slavic accent did not go unnoticed during an interview for the cult talk-show Larry King Live on CNN, when King hosted the Trumps, and their son Barron William appeared in the interview on a live link.

Melania supposedly speaks to Barron in Slovenian, at least in the privacy of their own home. This was first picked up by the American media, only then to be repeated in the Slovenian press. It is hard to believe how this can be true. Why would Melania Knauss insist on speaking in English to her old boyfriend from Slovenia, Jure Zorčič, ten years after she last saw him, and yet speak Slovenian at home?! A much more likely explanation is that all this is a PR stunt from Donald Trump's media and political advisers, related to his presidential campaign, where it is of utmost importance that his spouse and potential First Lady is presented to the American and global media in the best possible light.

During the discussion with Larry King, Melania Knauss also gave a strange explanation when she said her son has an accent because *"he spends most of the time with her."* It is rather odd for a mother to boast on national television that her son spends so much time in her company. What is more plausible is that it is Melania's parents Amalija and Viktor Knavs who speak Slovenian to Barron at home. They have been living in New York for quite some time and do not speak English. Barron also almost certainly speaks Slovenian with Melania's sister, his aunt Ines, who also lives in New York. It was Ines Knavs who took care of all the paperwork at the Slovenian Consulate in New York after her nephew's birth so that Barron Trump also acquired Slovenian citizenship, yet another piece of evidence that Melania Trump avoids anything connected with Slovenia. Melania did, however, once Barron had received his passport, briefly visit the consulate to thank them for their administrative work.

The Slovenian Consulate in New York was later closed, as the Slovenian Ministry of Foreign Affairs thought it too expensive to run in light of the financial crisis that also shook up the government budget. The Trump family was among the last to use it to sort out their consular matters.

Besides its embassy in Washington, D.C. and Slovenia's permanent mission to the UN, the only other Slovenian diplomatic mission in the US is its consulate in Cleveland, Ohio, at 55 Public Square, suite 945. It is in Cleveland that the largest population of US citizens with Slovenian roots live, mostly immigrants who moved to the States after the First and Second World Wars and their descendants. The running joke in Slovenia is that there are actually more Slovenians in Cleveland than in Ljubljana.

There was at least one occasion, however, when Melania Trump got involved in some charity work related to Slovenia; in September 2005, eight months after her prestigious wedding at Mar-a-Lago, she donated $25,000 to the health center in Sevnica. Raising funds for the medical center was a year-long charity drive, and the most money, more even than by Melania Trump, was contributed by two local companies and by a local choirmistress, Silvija Blaževič. The Municipality of Sevnica used the money to purchase a four-wheel drive vehicle for the town's midwife, fetal development monitors, and pediatric defibrillators.

As far as Melania Trump's charitable and humanitarian activities go, Melania's ex-classmate Mirjana Jelančič, today the principal of Sevnica's Savo Kladnik elementary school, recalls a conversation she had with Melania's mother Amalija while having coffee one day in August 2015. Amalija Knavs confided to Jelančič that she asked Melania what to do with the sweaters she used to wear as a child. Melania allegedly responded, "Throw them away!", to which her mother replied, "come home and throw them out yourself." Mirjana Jelančič then suggested a compromise in which the sweaters would be donated to the elementary school for a special exposition in honor of Melania Trump, Sevnica's most prominent person and brand.

Melania Knauss checked her watch and drank the last of her orange juice. When Zorčič wanted to pay he called over the waiter, but Melania just waved him off and he immediately discreetly retreated. Then Melania left and Zorčič knew he would never see her again. Well, never say never, of course.

Jure Zorčič was not the only nominally famous Slovenian to have dated Melania Knauss. Before him came Alen Kobilica, former and only Slovenian supermodel, a sort of Ljubljana version of Marcus Schenkenberg. Although some sources claim Alen Kobilica was Melania's manager, this is unlikely and not confirmed. Kobilica maintains that they were only partners in private, though, being discreet, he refuses to disclose any details or juicy facts about their romance.

In recent years Alen Kobilica has been dealing with a tragic personal story. An illness has caused him to go blind. Nonetheless he has launched a successful business in trendy nutritional products, he invented the Slovenian brand Indy&Pippa, which focuses on organic and vegan ice cream, and has even become an excellent athlete, focusing first on paraolympic swimming, and now the regular triathlon.

Melania's third companion was Gregor Erbežnik, known as Grega to his friends, Slovenian importer of the Quicksilver clothes brand and co-owner of Forma+, a sports shop at the largest mall in Ljubljana, BTC, which is, in terms of size, one of the biggest shopping centers in Europe. BTC is called "the little city of big buys." The romance between Gregor Erbežnik and Melania is even more complicated to sift through, as, at the time, Erbežnik was dating both Melania and his current wife, Nataša Erbežnik. His friends and acquaintances tell of him even visiting Melania in Milan and Paris, where she was working as a model. Interestingly though, he never left his girlfriend, now his wife, for Melania. It is not even known whether or not his current wife knew about Melania at the time, or whether Melania knew that Gregor was officially dating Nataša. Today, Gregor Erbežnik denies ever having an intimate relationship with Melanija. He says they were only friends, and that Melanija merely used him as a shoulder to cry when needed. He also maintains that Nataša knew of their friendship.

Another thing Erbežnik denies is supposedly having nude photographs of Melanija Knavs in particularly intimate poses or that he is planning on selling them. It is simply not true, he assured the author of this book, and even if he did possess such photos, he would never sell them. That Erbežnik has such photographs was allegedly suggested by Veljko Karas, a somewhat notorious Slovenian businessman and lobbyist who lives in Bled. Interestingly, Karas also had some business dealings with Peter Butoln, Melanija's first boyfriend. Karas is also one of those Ljubljana businessmen with expensive cars, mostly Mercedes, who would, years ago, drive them down to Sevnica for any maintenance and repairs by the mechanic Viktor Knavs, Melanija's father.

Understandably, Gregor Erbežnik is reluctant to discuss the particular circumstances of the love triangle between him, Melania and his wife Nataša, at least not with journalists. One thing we can bet is that now and again he must share a few secrets with his friend and business partner Jure Košir, Slovenia's second-best downhill skier ever, after Bojan Križaj.

Gregor Erbežnik and Jure Košir are co-owners of Forma+ and Jure's ex-wife and long term partner, the former model Alenka Košir, knows Melania from their modeling days together. Alenka Košir, then still Alenka Ružič, competed with Melanija Knavs at the first Slovenian Look of the Year competition in Portorož in 1992. Alenka is also rather unforthcoming with words when speaking about Melania, stating merely that they had *"worked together a few times,"* and that Melania was *"quiet, calm, focused on work, and never stood out."*

Jure and Alenka Košir have recently divorced and, after 21 years of marriage, their separation had the Slovenian tabloids abuzz. In dividing their assets, the Koširs also sold their attractive home in Bled, the only Slovenian town visited by Donald Trump.

The fourth famous Slovenian to have dated Melanija Knavs was the former soccer player Robert Robi Oblak. He played for Slovenian clubs such as Olimpija Ljubljana, Krka, Triglav, Rudar from Velenje, and then for a while in Cyprus, as well as in three official matches for the Slovenian national soccer team. He is the son of the famous Yugoslavian and best Slovenian soccer player Brane Oblak, who also played for the German team Bayern Munich. Robi Oblak is however not related to Jani Oblak, goalkeeper with the Spanish club Atlético Madrid and currently one of the best goalkeepers in the world. Robi Oblak was the owner of a bar in the Šiška area of Ljubljana, but remains silent about his relationship with the potential First Lady. All that is known is that they were a couple.

The fifth well known Slovenian to have had an intimate relationship with Melanija is Matjaž Meserko, the formerly financially successful businessman from Ljubljana, who even owned a Pershing yacht in the nascent days of Slovenian capitalism. Today he is a more modest entrepreneur rumored to have also accumulated considerable debts. It is Meserko himself who likes to brag and talk about his relationship with Melania in his inner social circle.

To round up this list we should also include the noteworthy claim by Gregor Erbežnik that Melanija Knavs actually never dated either Jure Zorčič or Peter Butoln, but was involved with someone entirely different who he knows but refuses to disclose. Peter Butoln also maintains that Melanija never dated Zorčič, and Zorčič says that Butoln is nothing but a poser. Butoln and Zorčič were actually classmates in Ljubljana's Poljane High School. Zorčič was in class D, Butoln in class B. Both of them, as well as Gregor Erbežnik, drove Vespa scooters.

Chapter 2

ROOTS

Slovenia is a small, young, central European parliamentary Republic. The country measures less than 8 thousand square miles (in terms of size it is 154th in the world), and received international recognition in 1991. It is a member of the European Union and NATO. You can drive through the length of it in a few hours. On the map the shape of its borders make it resemble a chicken, with its beak pecking at Hungary, its crown and back brushing up against Austria, its neck and front bordering Croatia, and its backside facing Italy. There are barely two million Slovenians, sharing origins with all the other members of the large Slavic family of nations like the Russians, Ukrainians, Belarusians, Poles, Czechs, Slovaks, Macedonians, Bosnians, Croatians and Serbians, not all of which are on the friendliest of terms among themselves; many having fought amongst themselves in bitter and brutal struggles marked by war crimes and bloody armed conflicts, some of which are still going on.

From the end of the Second World War in May of 1945, Slovenia was part of the communist, and starkly undemocratic, Yugoslavian Federation, led, until his death in 1980, by Josip Broz – Tito, the world famous dictator of Slovenian and Croatian origin who ruled from Belgrade, the Serbian and at the time Yugoslavian capital. His death marked the beginning of a ten-year long collapse, not only of the communist – socialist regime of Yugoslavia, but also the federation of its six constituent republics, Serbia, Macedonia, Croatia, Bosnia and Herzegovina, Montenegro, and Slovenia, as well as the two autonomous regions of Kosovo and Vojvodina. This was not brought about merely due to internal conflicts among Yugoslavia's member states and the inefficient communist handling of the economy, but also as a ripple effect of the dissolution of other communist regimes in Europe, especially the Soviet Union. One of the earliest globally recognizable events of this decline of European communism was the emergence of the Polish trade union movement *Solidarność* (Solidarity), and, nine years later, on 9 November 1989, the famous fall of the Berlin wall.

Slovenia's War of Independence lasted from 27 June to 7 July 1991, and after this Slovenia gained its independence, a parliamentary system, and international recognition, avoiding much of the bloodshed of the further break-up of Yugoslavia in the beginning of the 1990s.

Melanija Knavs, the young girl from Sevnica and future New Yorker Melania Trump was twenty years old at the time.

To geographically place Melania Trump's origin, the Sava River is an important landmark on any map. With its headwaters in the Slovenian mountains, the Sava runs nearly the whole length of the country, crossing the southeastern border with Croatia before continuing to flow on towards Serbia, where, at Belgrade it discharges into the Danube, the river made famous by Johann Strauss' waltz *By the Beautiful Blue Danube*. Both Melanija's mother Amalija, Malči for short, and her father Viktor, nicknamed Fif, come from the part of Slovenia on the right where the hills rise above the Sava, as it approaches the Slovenian-Croatian border.

Slovenia is dotted with tiny settlements and outlying villages, typical of which are the village of Raka where Melanija's mother Amalija's family, the Ulčniks, come from, and even more so the microscopic settlement of Jelovo (population of around 150), where the Knavses that include Melanija's father originated. This settlement lies at the top of a forest-covered hill and offers stunning views of the surrounding valleys, but to the rare and chance visitors who reach it, is seems as if they have arrived at the end of the world.

Jelovo has around fifty houses and a tiny church. The Knavses called home one of the densely packed houses on the very highest ridge in the village, where Melanija's great-grandfather Anton Knavs was born on 10 June 1874. Anton Knavs married Alojzija Bevk, three years younger than him, born on 13 May 1877 in the neighboring village of Sveti Jurij. They married in Jelovo church in November 1898 and had eight children, first-born Anton, their eldest girl Frančiška, then Jožef, who later became Melanija's grandfather, followed by Franc, Amalija, Marija, Julijana, and Kristina. Next to the house was a small amount of land, an orchard, a barn, a wooden granary, and a double hayrack. The house and its land lie abandoned today, though during Anton's childhood and that of his and Alojzija's children the house was abuzz with the jubilant pitter patter of little feet. Having so many children made it easier and cheaper to work the land

and tend to the animals. Melanija's grandfather Jožef Knavs, Anton and Alojzija's third child, was born on 3 March 1904, right there on the farm, like his brothers and sisters. When he had to go to school to the nearby larger settlement of Radeče it took him the better part of an hour on foot, with an even longer trip back, as it was straight up a steep and gully hill. If there was snowfall the children of Jelovo did not attend, as getting there on foot was simply impossible.

Melanija Knauss' family tree has grown and branched under six quite different state formations, the Austro-Hungarian Empire, the Kingdom of Yugoslavia, Nazi Germany, communist Yugoslavia, parliamentary Slovenia, and now the USA.

The land where Melanija's paternal line, the Knavses, and her maternal line, the Ulčniks, come from was ruled by the Austro-Hungarian Empire from 1867 right until the end of the First World War in 1918. The dominion of the union between Austria and Hungary spanned across many nations, among them also the Slovenians.

The monarchy, ruled by the Austrian Emperor or Empress, started the First World War after a Serbian youth activist, Gavrilo Princip, assassinated the Austro-Hungarian heir to the throne Franz Ferdinand and his wife, Czech Countess of Chotkov and Wognin, Sophie Chotek, in Sarajevo in 1814. After the four bloody years of war, a conflict that drew in all of Europe's superpowers and the USA, the big loser of the conflict, Austria-Hungary fell apart and Slovenia fell under the rule of the newly-formed Kingdom of the Serbs, Croats, and Slovenes, which in 1929 was renamed the Kingdom of Yugoslavia.

The unlucky fate of the Slovenian lands continued, as in April of 1941 the country was attacked by Hitler's Germany, and the occupied area divided up among the Germans, Italians, and Hungarians, although in terms of international law the Kingdom of Yugoslavia only ceased to exist in 1945.

From the blood and ashes of the war rose the communist Yugoslavian Federation that Slovenia was also part of. It lasted a few decades until breaking up at the beginning of the 1990s, when an independent and democratic country Slovenia was born from its ruins.

Well before Slovenia was an independent state, back in the early 1930s, in what was the Kingdom of Yugoslavia, on 6 September 1931, Melanija's grandfather Jožef Knavs slid a wedding ring onto the finger of his chosen bride Antonija. His wife came from an equally large family called Ribič from Mrtovec, another hillside settlement just over 5 miles from Jelovo. It was Antonija's family ties with the Jež family, which owned an inn and a small restaurant in the village of Jagnjenica in the valley below Jelovo, that proved crucial so the young couple were able to rent the restaurant and live and work there, starting their own family. This is where, during the Second World War, their third child Viktor, father of the future Melania Trump, was born. The restaurant on the road that connects Jagnjenica with civilization and where Melanija's grandparents lived and worked no longer exists. In its place is a nicely renovated residential house and locals still call it Knavs' house, even though there have been no Knavses living there for a long time, while Viktor

Knavs and his family perhaps occasionally check on it out on Google Maps from their apartment in Manhattan.

Upon leaving Jelovo for the valley, divided down the middle by the gushing brook called Sopota, you fall into the peaceful, idyllic pastoral village of Jagnjenica, which in English would translate as The Place of the Lambs. Though the village is but three miles from Radeče, the first nearby settlement of any substance, it gives you the impression you are on a deserted island, surrounded by hills overgrown with forests, where all the commotions of everyday life seem light-years away. Two major features in the center of the village are the church dedicated to Saint Margaret with a splendid spire, and of course the local inn, where locals spend their days chatting and gossiping over the obligatory glass of wine or beer. There are also plenty farm animals around, including cows, goats, sheep, and lambs, though they are not really heard. It seems the area's isolation also rubs off on the animals, silencing their usual bleating and mooing.

Of course, even this bucolic piece of heaven on earth is not immune to tragedy, a fact that Jožef Knavs' family learned firsthand. After their marriage in Jelovo, Jožef and Antonija Knavs came down to this delightful small village, with its fertile fields and abundant pastures, and threw themselves into running the restaurant. Jožef also soon found a job as a line worker in a high-quality paper factory nearby, soon rising through the ranks to become manager, while his wife Antonija ran the restaurant. Jožef helped her as much as he could. Antonija was, her youngest son Herman Knavs, uncle of the future Melanija, tells us, an industrious woman who knew how to take a dollar and instantly turn it into two.

It must be from this grandmother that Melanija inherited the knack she has for forging her almost unbelievable dream journey in life, marked by her leap from a tiny, rural Slovenian village to the cosmopolitan and economic megacenter of New York, with the added possibility of serious political clout in the US and through the rest of the world.

Jožef and Antonija Knavs had their first son Joško in 1932. Melanija never got to meet this oldest paternal uncle, as he died before she was born. Then, as in some cases still now, is traditional in these religious farming families that the first son is named after the father, and this family was no exception, as Joško is the diminutive of Jožef. The life of Jožef and Antonija Knavs' firstborn, who was an exuberant, happy little boy, a true copy of his father, who also played accordion just as well as his father, soon ended tragically. On 4 July 1940, just before Joško was about to start his second grade at the local school and the Second World War which Hitler began with an unannounced attack on Poland, had already been raging across the continent for ten months, the young Knavs was playing without a care in the world, chasing two friends along the Sopota stream, specifically along a small pool formed by a wooden dam above a nearby water powered sawmill. There was a pile of logs and yet to be processed trunks stored on the slope above it, waiting to be sawed up. The children's innocent game took them to the stack of logs, and Joško, apparently the bravest of the boys, started climbing up to the top of the pile with ease. One of the heavy trunks, however, became dislodged and rolled onto him, hitting his head and knocking him out immediately, with blood gushing from his deep wound. The county doctor Karl Matek was called but all he was able to do was pronounce the unlucky Joško dead. Joško had been the smartest and keenest student in his first-grade class. His parents, especially his mother Antonija, Melanija's grand-mother, never fully recovered from this shock. She also lost her innate joy, relaxedness, and generally lively nature, and the death may have contributed to her own death at the relatively young age of sixty-six. Joško was buried by his mourning parents in nearby Radeče, because there was and still is no cemetery in Jagnjenica. It is odd, though, that the newly erected headstone on the Knavs family grave incor-rectly lists the year of Joško's death as 1939 instead of 1940.

The Second World War that had already been raging for a year at Joško's tragic death, finally caught up with the Kingdom of Yugoslavia, which Slovenia was part of at the time, less than a year later. Nazi planes, without an of-ficial declaration of war, attacked the Yugoslavian capital Belgrade at 6:30 AM on 6 April 1941. The short April War between the Kingdom of Yugoslavia and Hitler's Germany lasted only from 6 to 17 April, when the Yugoslav Army surrendered unconditionally. The Kingdom thus fell in a pa-thetic eleven days, and Slovenia was carved up by Hungary, Fascist Italy and Nazi Germany.

Jagnjenica and nearby Radeče, the location of the paper factory where Melanija's grandfather Jožef Knavs worked, were occupied by the Germans just three days after the start of the war. This was followed only a few months later by the forceful relocation of Slovenians, especially thoroughly from villages close to the territory occupied by Italian forces.

Jožef Knavs and his wife Antonija avoided almost certain deportation because Jožef worked at the paper factory which was considered of strategic importance by the Nazis.

The Ulčnik family, of which Melanija's mother Amalija is a descendant, was not so lucky, as they fled the German occupiers and remained, for a little over four years, in the Austrian town of Judendorf-Strassengel.

The Nazis swiftly introduced the German language and Germanized people's names and surnames, later extending this to local place names as well. The residents of the occupied land could only use the German variation, which is why Melanija's father, who was born on 23 November 1941 in Jagnjenica, was therefore listed on his birth certificate as Knaus, not Knavs, and Waldemar instead of Viktor. He reversed to his original name Viktor Knavs only after the end of Nazi occupation. When, however, in the 1990s he opened his own business, despite his bitter childhood experience, he named it Knaus-Haus, thus once again, this time of his own will, Germanizing his Slovenian family name. His daughter Melanija did a similar thing when she embarked upon her career in modeling and fashion, changing her name into the more prestigious-sounding Knauss, leading to several false claims in the media that Melanija was not of Slovenian but of Austrian origin.

Melania's grandmother Antonija became pregnant with Viktor just before the German invasion of the Kingdom of Yugoslavia. Despite the clouds of war gathering, the young couple was thrilled with the arrival of a new healthy boy, something that was not taken for granted during those difficult times. Many children died during childbirth, either due to unhygienic conditions or weakened mothers, mostly as a result of poor nutrition. Women at the time also usually gave birth at home, mostly even without the presence of midwives. Antonija giving birth to her son Waldemar, later Viktor, in Jagnjenica, right above the restaurant that she owned with her husband Jožef was no different.

Waldemar is an old German name, and the parents believed giving him a German name would keep him safer in the German occupation. They did the same with Viktor's younger brother Hermann, also a very German-sounding name. Hermann was born on 17 April 1944 in the apartment in Radeče where the family moved to during the war. The name was almost certainly inspired by Hermann Göring, Hitler's named successor. After the defeat of Germany, Hermann dropped the last N from his name to make the spelling more Slovenian, Waldemar was changed to Viktor, and the whole family changed their name back to the Slovenian form Knavs though on official documents their name sometimes still appears as Knaus until the 1950s.

Hermann (later Herman) was, after Waldemar (later Viktor) and their firstborn Joško, Jožef and Antonija's third and final child. Both Herman and Viktor had two children each in wedlock. Herman and his wife Danijela had a daughter Karmen, born in 1968, and a son Sandi, born in 1976, while Viktor and his wife Amalija had two daughters Ines and Melanija.

The potential First Lady of the United States, Melania so far only has one son, Barron William Trump, though her husband Donald has been much more prolific, with a total of five children from his three wives Ivana, Marla Maples, and Melania: three boys, Donald Jr., Eric, and Barron William, and two girls, Ivanka and Tiffany. Donald Trump has said that having kids keeps him young and fills him with fresh energy.

Melanija's father Viktor Knavs, still Knaus at that point, picked up his school backpack on 3 September 1948, just before turning 7, and left for his first day at school in the town of Radeče. At the time Radeče had a population of 414 men and 557 women, with a total of 3,420 souls including all the surrounding villages. Immediately after the end of the Second World War the new authorities opened a new school in Viktor's native Jagnjenica, but since the family had moved to a dank single-room apartment in Radeče, his father decided to send Viktor to school near the new family home.

All this happened just before the eruption of a horrific political argument between until then two of the world's grand communist allies, Tito and Stalin, which almost led to war between Yugoslavia and the Soviet Union. The conflict abated, but Slovenian citizens, including the Knavses in Radeče, felt tension and anxiety until Stalin's death in March 1953, after which relations between the two Communist states slowly started to improve.

Viktor left the elementary school in Radeče in June 1956 after eight years on its benches, where he had an extraordinarily varied amount of success. Finishing his first year with straight As, his next three years he was a B and C student, his performance during his final three years was very poor. He received satisfactory marks in sixth grade, unsatisfactory marks in seventh grade, and barely managed to scrape his way to passing his eighth grade, performing abysmally in both Slovenian language and Calculus with Geometry, what we would today call Math.

Due to his deficient grades in both Slovenian and German, and his unsatisfactory overall performance in seventh grade, Viktor had to have extra lessons over the summer, and was relieved to pass his retakes. Despite his poor academic record, his behavior was excellent and he never had any unexcused absences. Viktor was also more or less exemplary in Physical Education, good at Singing, Drawing, Handwriting, Natural History, and Geography, very mixed in History and Serbo-Croatian, and outright poor in Chemistry, Physics, Calculus and Geometry, German, and Slovenian. Nonetheless he was gifted in working with his hands during workshop classes in his second and third grades. Teachers noted that for his age he was, "poorly developed, slow-thinking, and bad at math," but was otherwise "punctual, open-hearted, dependable, calm, and hard-working," though he "showed too little interest and commitment and studied only when he had a test coming up." They also remarked that his home upbringing was "good and beneficent to the child."

Melanija's uncle Herman went to the Radeče Elementary School three years after his older brother Viktor and was a terrible student. He had to re-sit his exams four times, after second, fourth, sixth and eighth grades. Nonetheless he did finish fifth grade with Bs, suggesting that he could have been successful had he tried harder. His behavior had also always been excellent except in his eighth or final year, also earning three fails in Slovenian, Serbo-Croatian, and History, and earning just a B for behavior. He also only had two unexcused hours of absence in eight years of school.

Herman was very well developed for his age. His teachers were not quite in agreement about his personal characteristics, some calling him "lazy, stubborn, unkempt, very sloppy, and ungifted," while others saying he was "punctual, polite, and dependable." All, however, agreed that he was "friendly, sociable, and with a well-developed sense of collective." Of his parents the teachers remarked that, "they look after his upbringing and education and are interested in his development." Basically the school reports show that his upbringing was "correct and his family relationships very positive," though perhaps his parents had "too little influence on him" and that he sometimes "failed to obey them".

Although during the war the German occupiers relocated around eighty percent of the population of Radeče and its surroundings, the Knavs family headed by Melanija's grandfather avoided this fate, as Jožef worked in the Radeče paper factory. This factory has a long tradition in the region, with records showing its entry into the Viennese judicial-commercial register back in 1736, although industrialized paper production was only introduced at the beginning of the 20th century. That was when the world-famous playing card manufacturers, the Ferdinand brothers, Adolf and Rudolf Piatnik from Vienna, took over the factory, introducing in 1939 cardboard production and production of high-quality papers, including those for playing cards and official documents.

When on 9 April 1941, three days after Hitler's attack on the Kingdom of Yugoslavia, German tanks came arrogantly rumbling into Radeče, the occupiers went straight into business with the Piatnik brothers, and the director of the paper factory, Mr. Rak, having already previously shown himself as an ardent Nazi sympathizer, was now appointed Mayor of Radeče, so the factory was able to uninterruptedly continue producing its high-quality paper products. It was due to the paper factory's strategic importance for the Nazis that the Slovenian factory workers and their families avoided being relocated by the authorities.

With the resistance movement however continually creating diversions, specifically, stealing paper and delivering it to the Partisans, Jožef Knavs who was at the time only an ordinary factory worker, was several times hauled off for questioning by the SS, the Nazi regime's most nefarious and dangerous organization, to the local administrative town of Trbovlje. There Jožef was questioned and beaten, and was always saved from prison by Elizabeta Jež, Antonija's relative from the Jež inn in Jagnjenica. Members of the notorious SS often stayed at her inn, setting up an informal base there, and she was always able to convince them to let Jožef go, saying that he had small children and a wife, who was home alone.

At the time of liberation, the Knavs family was living in a small, humid, one-bedroom apartment in Radeče, house number 96. After the war, Jožef Knavs was promoted to factory manager, and in December 1951 began building a one-story family house in the nearby settlement of Njivice, which is today part of Radeče. It took him six years to finish, and then he had to wait until April 1957 to get the official permits for the building, even though the family had already moved in. At last, the Knavses were living on their own, in a house that was not plagued by dampness and drafts.

The family house, however, the first safe and proper home of the Knavses and their two sons, was not built under a fortunate sign. When Melanija's grandfather died on 10 January 1989, and with his wife Antonija having died more than fifteen years earlier, on 27 April 1973, bad blood emerged between the brothers Viktor and Herman, father and uncle of the future Melania Trump. The root of the problem was the very house that their mother and father had been so overjoyed to move into, and which is today of course much different to the one the Knavses built in the 1950s. Currently living there is Herman's forty-year old son Sandi Knavs, ensuring that the Knavs surname will continue on Herman's branch of the family tree, while Herman's daughter Karmen, Melania Trump's cousin, lives on the upper floor of the house that Herman and his wife built right next to the Sava River on Starograjska ulica, the oldest street in Radeče.

Years of lawsuits and court procedures, which in Slovenia move at a snail's pace – statistics also showing that Slovenians have made lawsuits something of a hobby – have caused a rift in the Knavs brothers' relationship, though they had always gotten along well until then. Herman used to help his parents around the house with day-to-day repairs and gardening, Viktor less so, as he had moved away to Sevnica. His younger brother understandably felt duped, especially given that he had also paid off Viktor for his share with a substantial amount of money.

Viktor Knavs refused to give in and filed lawsuit for the family house, which was officially evaluated by the Slovenian Surveying and Mapping Authority at a paltry $45,000, even though he had in the meantime become the father-in-law of billionaire real-estate mogul Donald Trump. Upon being sued by his elder brother, Herman complained that

Viktor could *"never get enough"* and that he was *"too big for his britches"*.

While Herman, after finishing elementary school, chose a vocational school for the wood industry, and later, as so many other Yugoslavians, briefly went to work in Germany as a "Gastarbeiter," as the Germans call migrant workers, Viktor became an apprentice in the car repair service workshop at the paper factory in Radeče. He received his professional car mechanic certificate after completing his apprenticeship and passing the necessary theoretical and practical exams on 11 November 1959, just twelve days before his 18th birthday. In the same year he also passed his driver's license test and then went to complete his mandatory military service in the Yugoslav National Army where, among other duties, he also served as a vehicle operator. After his return from the military service he passed the professional driver exam and became a full-time employee in Radeče Paper Factory. On 1 February 1964 he got a job as a driver and a caretaker at the municipality of Hrastnik. Among others he also chauffeured the Mayor of Hrastnik.

At the age of sixteen, specifically on 31 December 1957, Viktor also received his ID card, which, like everyone else at the time, he was obliged to carry on his person at all times from puberty onwards, so that the police or other authorities could identify, legitimized, and otherwise verify the details of all citizens. In theory this was to protect the public good, but in reality it was to protect the political security of the totalitarian regime and its leaders.

Later, Viktor Knavs made his way to Maribor, the second biggest Slovenian city, which lies in the northeast of

Slovenia near the border with Austria, with the intent of studying. He enrolled in a two-year college program at the Higher School of Law, which opened its doors in 1960. This school is today referred to as The Faculty of Law. However, it was a degree that Viktor Knavs did not finish, a fact that is also revealed by his former mistress Alenka.

What Viktor did not know at the time was that his employment in Hrastnik would, more than fifty years later, have consequences and become a serious issue in Melania Trump's family and her husband Donald's election campaign. It has emerged that Melania has at least one more, so far relatively well hidden, half brother, whose existence the Slovenian and American public did not even knew about. What is also a big unknown is how and when exactly Donald Trump became aware of the existence of another member of Melania's family. There is a whole series of testimonies that indicate that the existence of Melania Trump's half brother, 51 year-old Denis Cigelnjak, today an employee of the supermarket chain Mercator, was kept hidden from Melania and her sister Ines for several decades by Amalija and Viktor Knavs. It is also said that Viktor initially hid the birth of Denis from his wife Amalija as well, but not from his second mistress Alenka. In an ultimately futile attempt, as the truth was bound to come out sooner or later, in the end the entire Knavs family tried to hide the fact from Donald Trump. It was first made public in an article written by the American journalist of Russian descent Julia Ioffe, published in the *GQ* Magazine in April 2016.

Denis Cigelnjak today lives in Hrastnik, in an apartment block where you can still deeply sense the legacy of decades of socialism. His mother, the now deceased Marija Cigeln-jak, who worked as a cleaning lady in Hrastnik's municipal offices where Viktor Knavs was the mayor's chauffeur, told Viktor that she was pregnant in 1964. Melania Trump's father supposedly initially offered marriage but soon changed his mind and demanded that Marija has an abortion. Later on he even denied paternity in a court of law. Denis Cigel-njak was born in May 1965 and his mother Marija filed a lawsuit against Viktor for child support.

"My mother didn't agree to the abortion and kept me instead. She wanted nothing from my father because her disappointment and disillusion were just too high. However, grandmother convinced her to at least ask Viktor for child support," Denis Cigelnjak said in a statement made to the Slovenian Planet TV network in May 2016. He also presented the child support documents.

Viktor Knavs fought the paternity claims in court and the whole legal procedure was tainted with cruel, brutal and unnecessarily intimate statements, as Viktor in his defense also used private details such as Marija Cigelnjak's menstrual cycle. A paternity test finally confirmed Marija's claims and Viktor eventually, after exhausting all possible legal venues, began paying child support. He never saw his son but paid child support until Denis was eighteen years old. His payments were not always regular and the court was forced to send him legal warnings on a number of occasions.

Denis has lived in Hrastnik for the past twenty-one years with his partner Maja. They have an eight-year-old daughter Mimi. He says he has never lacked anything in life and lived in complete anonymity until the publication of the GQ article. Everything he has was given to him by his mother and his aunts and uncles, but he did say he would once like to have a meal or a drink with his father, his famous half sister Melania, and Ines. He wants nothing from his father but that does not mean that he would not have liked to meet him. He is not pushy on the issue of meeting up with his father, and even though they share the same blood he has reconciled with the fact he has simply gone his own way, however, he does *"find it odd that someone would simply deny their own child."*

Denis Cigelnjak was also under the impression that until the media revelation Melania was unaware of his existence. Initially, she denied the claims of an illegitimate half brother for GQ magazine but quickly changed her story after Julia Ioffe presented her with legal documentation from the Slovenian court. She then stated that she had known about her half brother for a very long time but asks the media to respect her father's privacy because her father is not a public figure. The revelation created quite a bit of tension between Ms. Ioffe and Trump' presidential campaign, as Trump supporters began to openly threaten the journalist on social media, a turn of events that allegedly also led to the police getting involved.

What is interesting about this revelation however, is how it first became public. The authors of this book, Bojan Požar and Igor Omerza, found out about Denis Cigenjak in mid-March 2016, two weeks after the first edition of the e-book *Melania Trump: The Inside Story* was first published on Amazon. The release of the book encouraged American journalists to begin investigating the life and family of the potential First Lady Melania Trump. The story about Mrs. Trump's secret half brother was already in the works by the authors and was set to be published in the upcoming extended print edition of the book. They were also preparing for a secret meeting with Cigelnjak. However, *GQ* magazine rushed the story and published it first. It appears that Julia Ioffe discovered the existence of Cigelnjak completely by accident from Roman Leljak, publisher and known Slovenian investigator of the archives of the former Yugoslavian secret police known as Udba. Leljak is also a former employee of the infamous Yugoslavian military counter intelligence agency with an acronym KOS. When and where Ioffe met Leljak is not exactly known, but it supposedly happened in Zagreb. After the publication of the article that revealed Cigelnjak's existence and his connection to the Knavses and the Trumps, Leljak proudly boasted to friends about how he had been the source of the story.

Soon after Roman Leljak told Ioffe about the secret half brother and the story became public, the source that brought the authors to Denis Ciglenjak, informed them that Cigelnjak no longer wished to meet with them. The reason for this turn of events probably lies in the fact that *GQ* paid Ciglenjak for the exclusive and therefore Ciglenjak could no longer speak to other journalists.

There was one other person who knew about Mr. Cigelnjak long before Julia Ioffe or the authors of this book and that is a journalist from a Slovenian television network TV Planet Anja Marković, a longtime friend of his partner Maja and who also stems from Hrastnik. Why, if she knew about it, was she not the first to publish the story which would have made a first-rate exclusive piece is partly typical of the quality of Slovenian journalism. She had, however, still been hopeful that the story would eventually become public. Once Ioffe published the *GQ* article, Markovič was the only Slovenian journalist to get an exclusive interview and peek into the lives of Denis and Maja. She turned herself into their public relations contact and even took a few photographs that were, with Denis' and Anja's permission of course, published by other Slovenian media outlets. When we asked Ms. Markovič before publishing this book, whether she had previously truly known about Denis' relation to Melania Trump, she began offering unconvincing excuses about having not really known, but how supposedly "all of Hrastnik" knew of it. Well, according to her, everyone except her mother, who, by the way, still lives in Hrastnik?!

Anja Markovič had promised that Denis Cigelnjak, whose mobile number is kept secret from journalists but whose regular number can be found in the phonebook, even though he refuses to pick up the phone out of caution, would call us before the publication of this book. He never did. We can only assume it is because he is bound to keep silent by his agreement over payment he received from *GQ* magazine for an exclusive.

One of Melania Trump's relatives has confided in us after the Denis Cigelnjak story became public, that the rest of the family only found out about his existence a mere six months ago and that they knew nothing of it before that. Moreover, this same relative also confirmed that the wider Knavs and Ulčnik families are generally not comfortable with questions regarding Melania's life. After the discovery of the secret half brother, Melania's sister Ines wrote an insensitive Facebook post regarding the paternity test, stating the latter was more than necessary as Denis' mother Marija was known "to get around." The statement can be described as highly inappropriate, considering the wider circumstances and the fact that Marija Cigelnjak is already deceased.

The shadows of Viktor Knavs' past, however, continue to haunt him. Soon after the Denis Cigelnjak affair appeared to quieten down, another person from Viktor's former life told her story in a Slovenian tabloid magazine *Suzy*. Alenka, whose last name remains anonymous but is known to the editors at *Suzy*, is Viktor Knavs' former mistress. First she crushed any illusions one might have about Viktor's education, insinuating that he had not even finished high school. He was supposed to take admission exams for law school in Maribor where they met, but never passed them. *"Viktor liked that his wife Amalija worked as a seamstress, because she was quiet and calm. She never held his silly outbursts against him. He had had many women and then became involved with me as well. I was a divorced, single mother with a son but I knew he was married. I believed him back then,"* Alenka said for the magazine *Suzy*. Alenka was allegedly Viktor's mistress for seven whole years and their affair began when Melanija was only five years old and her sister Ines was seven.

"He never cared too much about his daughters," Alenka says today. They had spent a number of New Year's Eves together, while his actual family remained alone in their apartment. *"Amalija Knavs worked all day and he was never home. He would leave in the morning, came back in the afternoon to change and then leave again. Amalija took care of everything on her own and Melanija and Ines were, more often than not, left to fend for themselves. He was never a caring father,"* says Viktor Knavs' now 66-year-old former mistress.

Eventually their relationship turned sour. *"I became pregnant and had to have an abortion. Viktor had some connections at the hospital in Brežice and made all the arrangements without ever even discussing it."* Alenka suffered serious complications and consequences after the abortion but says she does not regret having it, convinced that Viktor would have made a lot of fuss had she kept the baby. Alenka supposedly also knew all about Denis, Viktor's illegitimate son. Viktor told Alenka everything then, including that his wife Amalija did not know of Denis' existence and more specifically about how he was involved a bitter paternity and child support suit.

After Alenka had her abortion and a potential child was no longer an issue, Viktor stopped showing up for a while. He then appeared, wanting to continue their relationship. Alenka had had enough and moved abroad for 30 years. She never saw or heard from Viktor again, but her friends did inform her that after her departure Viktor began a relationship with another woman, this time from Ljubljana. She does not hold Viktor Knavs, who will turn 75 in November 2016, in high regards and dismissively suggested that he has recently been living at the expense of his five years younger son-in-law Donald Trump.

But what was happening with Viktor Knavs' chauffeuring career? As already mentioned he became the driver to the Mayor of Hrastnik in February 1964. Two years later, on 1 April 1966, he moved to the neighboring municipality of Trbovlje, where he worked for two years as the personal driver to the local mayor there too. His next driving assignment was at the Jutranjka factory, where in April 1968 he began driving the Director of this, for Slovenian standards relatively large textile factory, until he was dismissed around fourteen months later.

The state-owned socialist company Jutranjka was later also extremely important for the future Melania Trump, as the seven-year old Melanija actually got her first modeling assignment there.

After his involuntary dismissal from Jutranjka, where his wife Amalija was also employed, Viktor Knavs became a car and motorcycle salesman, which ultimately led to him to working as a salesman at Slovenija Avto, one of the country's largest companies. He also worked for the motor factory Tomos and the commercial company Trgoavto. When in the late 1980s, in the dying days of Yugoslavia's socialist era, it became possible for private citizens to open a business, Viktor founded Knaus-Haus, a limited liability company with its headquarters in Ljubljana. The company was registered 16 January 1991. Its main activities were in distributing and selling mopeds and motorcycle gear, though it was also registered as a textile producer and an industrial design company.

The German word "Haus" simply means "house" in English, and the name's catchy little rhyme shows that Viktor Knavs seems to have been in a somewhat poetic mood when naming his enterprise. Knaus-Haus was not just a company, but also included a sales outlet where Viktor sold his mopeds and spare parts, just outside of the city centre in Ljubljana. Neither the company nor the store exists today, and both were already erased from the official Slovenian registry of companies by 2004. The store has for some years now been a bar.

According to the latest data obtained from the Slovenian court register it is evident that the company Knauss-Haus existed even up to 2006, but that for the last two years of its existence its owner was listed as Melania Knauss, using her maiden name even though she was already married to Donald Trump by then. As the sole owner of the company registered in Ljubljana, Melania Trump listed Glinškova ploščad 20 as its official address, despite the fact that she had been living in New York as a naturalized American for quite some time by then and since January 2005, also as Donald Trump's wife. We can also see in the court documents that Viktor Knavs remained the director or CEO of the company up until its closure. However, the reason why he transferred ownership to his youngest daughter Melania, remains a mystery.

Viktor Knavs is now retired now and appears a little conceited, though it is true that he was like that before, too. He spends most of his time with Melania in New York but still has a large Mercedes parked alongside an old-timer, also a Mercedes, in front of his house in Sevnica, showing that his affinity for cars has not abandoned him, and that, as in his youth, he is still a big fan of classic cars.

Viktor Knavs was a relatively competent entrepreneur, a fact attested by his ownership of a three bedroom apartment in Sevnica with his wife Amalija, a two bedroom apartment in Ljubljana, which first they rented and then bought, and then in the 1990s the house that he built and completed in Sevnica. He adored cars and had already bought his first car – a Mercedes, of course, a brand he remained faithful to – even before he went to his military service, while his father Jožef never even held a driving license, preferring instead to use a bicycle. Having a car was a real attraction in Viktor's youth, as there were very few privately-owned cars in Slovenia in those days, let alone a prestigious car such as a Mercedes. When Viktor left for his mandatory military service (all Slovenian males born before 1982 were required to serve in the army), his car was used by his younger brother Herman. Viktor, it seems, had always had a knack for making money, even though there have been rumors recently about him having trouble with the Slovenian tax authorities and even the police back in those days. He never lost his love for cars and as well as his Mercedes also owned a used Maserati for a while.

Before their argument over their inheritance, Herman and Viktor had always been great friends, and were known for carousing around at all the local hootenannies and village celebrations, the usual and best way in rural Slovenia at the time for meeting young ladies and making new friends. Herman sometimes reminisces in his circle of friends about his exploits and "chasing skirts" with Viktor.

It was probably at one of these village events, at some point around 1966, that the first spark was kindled between the twenty-four-year old limo driver Viktor Knavs and the four year younger seamstress Amalija Ulčnik. They were married soon after in July of the following year, with a religious ceremony following in October. Amalija Ulčnik, mother to the future Mrs. Trump, took her husband's last name and became Amalija Knavs.

The Ulčnik family originates from the village of Raka, which lies on the slopes of hills above the river Sava, close to the Croatian border. Raka is about 20 miles southeast of Jagnjenica, Viktor Knavs' home. The residents of Raka and its surroundings – close to 2,000 in numbers today – have traditionally been predominantly farmers, with the exception of a few craftsmen. Onions are the main local agricultural product, with livestock and vineyards also abundant. Today many locals are employed in nearby towns and tend to the animals and fields in the afternoons and weekends. Raka's culinary specialty is the local red onion, famous enough for the locals have created the *Č'bularska pot*, the "Onion Farmers' Trail," which connects Raka with a number of neighboring villages.

The village center is dominated by the imposing church of St. Lawrence with its two majestic bell towers. Its location and design almost invite people toward it. Slightly below the church sits a castle, one of the oldest in southeastern Slovenia. There used to be a large pond here, where the lords and ladies of the castle would take their feudal guests on boat trips. The early inhabitants of Raka were Germans, and the Slovenians moved in when the Germans left.

The elementary school in Raka was opened in 1800, before that, children were educated in temporary rooms in rented buildings. A good 100 years later in 1902 a new school building was built, and this is where Melania's mother Amalija as well as many other maternal relatives attended school.

Though Raka is accessible from four directions by well-maintained roads, and nearby major towns are only 10 to

20 miles away, this forested and hilly region gives you the feeling of extreme isolation and remoteness from the rest of the world, as well as an air of self-sufficiency. Nevertheless, Raka is still far more open than Jagnjenica, Melania's father's birthplace.

Melania's maternal grandmother and grandfather lived on a farm, house number 51, on the road heading out of Raka to the south, later moving to number 62. Melania's grandfather was a cobbler, and her grandmother a seamstress, and the couple – like so many other families in Raka – also farmed onions and other vegetables.

Anton Ulčnik, Melania's grandfather, was actually not a local. He was born 9 January 1910 in a tiny little village called Podob outside the town of Loče, some 45 miles north of Raka. His father, also Anton Ulčnik, died soon after he was born, and Melanija's great-grandmother Marjeta, née Petelinc, remarried and took her new husband's name Cugmas. Anton Ulčnik Jr. went to elementary school in Loče, wavering between excellent and very good grades. Due to his father's death, he was assigned a guardian during his school years. This guardian was, Jožef Štefanič, a local cobbler, so it is not surprising that the young Anton also went into shoe making. As a seventeen-year-old cobbler's apprentice, he moved to Raka to work for a cobbler named Mladič, and worked there as an assistant until the outbreak of the Second World War.

In Raka he met the local girl Amalija Gliha, born on 9 April 1913, later marrying her and starting with her the large Ulčnik family, also looking after his wife's mother and a number of aunts. All the Ulčniks in Raka today originate from this one family.

Anton and Amalija had eight children, just as many as Melania's paternal great-grandmother and great-grandfather. Most of the children were born at home, in Raka, in the following order: first Željko Anton in October 1935, then Ida in January 1937, who died shortly after birth, then Stanislav in August 1938, then another Ida in September 1939, Olga in October 1943, and on 9 of July 1945, two months after the end of the Second World War, Melanija's mother was born and named after her own mother Amalija. She was not Anton and Amalija Ulčnik's last child; her mother had a miscarriage in March 1946, followed by two more children, Marija in October 1949 and Franci in April 1952.

Olga and Amalija were not born in Raka like all the other Ulčnik children, but in Judendorf-Strassengel near the Austrian town of Graz, which, following Hitler's annexation of Austria during the war, was a part of the Hitler's Third Reich. During the occupation of Yugoslavia in 1941, the village of Raka fell under Nazi administration. The Germans forcibly removed almost all of Raka's population, along with the population of surrounding villages, to make room for the so-called *Gottscheers*, Slovenian Germans who before the war had lived further south in the most forested part of Slovenia around what is today the town of Kočevje, which fell under Italian control and its inhabitants were forced to resettle to the German areas. The exiles were only allowed to take with them whatever they could carry, but no more than 110 lbs. Of the pre-war locals, only eleven families were allowed to remain in Raka, while a handful of residents managed to escape to the part of the country that was under the milder Italian occupation.

Anton and Amalija Ulčnik must have realized that they lived in an area from which the Nazis would deport people to work camps. They also knew that such camps were physically and mentally excruciating, and that the Nazis often even broke families up. Wanting to avoid such a fate, Anton went on a 'reconnaissance mission' to find a good place where they could voluntary move to from Raka. He already knew of Judendorf-Strassengel, as the area supported a cobbling industry, making it a logical choice for him, so he went there and made all the necessary living and working arrangements. There were no internal borders between Raka and Judendorf-Strassengel at the time, as both were located within the territory of the Third Reich. Soon after he moved the entire family to Judendorf-Strassengel, taking all the children with him, as well as everything they could carry. Anton drove their horse-drawn wagon to the nearby town of Krško, from where they took the train for the 200 mile journey to Judendorf-Strassengel. Only three days after they had left (!), the Germans occupied Raka, dispersing the population to various labor camps.

For the duration of their stay in Judendorf-Strassengel Anton Ulčnik worked as a cobbler, and his wife Amalija took care of the family and continued to work as a seamstress. Mostly she sewed for her family, but she also did some work for other residents in the area. The children born back in Raka (Željko, Anton, Stanislav, and Ida) were sent to school in Judendorf. This school was, of course, German. Nonetheless, Anton and Amalija realized how important education was for their children's future, and sent all of them to school. Since the family was not in a labor camp, their life continued more or less normally in the Third Reich, further proven by the fact that they further expanded their family with Olga and Amalija born in exile.

It is interesting to note that there actually was a Nazi camp in Judendorf-Strassengel. It was not an execution camp; rather it was a small labor camp called *"lager"* in German, where workers were housed in simple barracks. The camp was built next to the train station, at the foot of a hill where one still finds the beautiful Maria Strassengel Pilgrimage Church with an associated monastery. This Gothic church was built in the 14th century. The labor camp was set up around a cement plant, where detainees were used as a free labor force. The cement plant still stands, protected as a monument, and is one of the area's most interesting buildings. The wooden camp barracks surrounding it are no longer there. In their place stand the warehouses and production facilities of a new chemical plant.

After the war, in May 1945, Anton decided it was high time to see how things were in his old home, and whether or not their house in Raka was still standing. What awaited him was a scene similar to what many others witnessed upon their return; the contents of their home had been pillaged and outside was desolate, yet the future Melania Trump's grandfather was nonetheless happy to see that it had not been demolished. He checked what needed fixing before the family could return home and informed the family of the happy news as they waited for him in Judendorf-Strassengel. He promised he would come to collect them soon and in

March 1946 the whole family, now with the addition of two baby girls born in Austria, returned to their true home in Raka. The journey was rough, especially for Amalija, who was pregnant and miscarried en route. This was unsurprising, as such journeys took their toll even on the healthiest of people, but for a pregnant woman it was simply too much. Amalija, however, was a strong woman, and, just as she had gotten over the death of her first daughter Ida, she got over this miscarriage and went on to give birth to another two healthy children.

When the residents of Raka returned to their abandoned and pillaged houses after the war, they quickly started working on repairing the buildings and tending to the neglected fields and vineyards. Many people had died in the labor camps, and several more died in scuffles with the occupiers. But life goes on, and the elementary school in Raka re-opened its doors to pupils only a month after the fall of Nazi Germany on 11 June 1945.

The children soon began to fill their seats at school, even though it was early summer. Anton returned to his cobbling, and Amalija took over the house again and continued her sewing. Once again fruit and vegetables were grown in the garden. They did not run into any problems with the new communist authorities, which were, after the end of the war, tireless in their pursuit, imprisonment, and mass execution of real, potential, or even just imagined political enemies (there was no such thing as opposition for the Communists), as they were largely apolitical and had fled the country, and consequently could not be accused of any sort of collaboration with the Nazis.

None of Melania Trump's ancestors, either on her maternal or paternal side, joined the partisan resistance movement but they also had no part in those Slovenian factions that allied themselves with Hitler against the communist partisans. None of the Knavses or Ulčniks were killed or shot as hostages during the Second World War.

Things generally always worked out for Anton Ulčnik Sr.; even before the war he opened, in addition to his shoe business in Ribnica, a town that, especially in those days, could not really be considered close to Raka, a fruit and vegetable store with products that he and his family grew. The ravines in Raka are covered with fertile topsoil, there was also plenty manure from the animals they kept, and the area is positioned so that it catches the morning sun which stays above it all day, giving the plants much-needed warmth and light.

After the war, Anton started working again immediately, as there was much to be done; a large family brought large responsibilities, and he decided to open his own shoemaking business. He worked on a contract for a shoe factory in Novo Mesto making industrial shoes, and also kept animals and worked the land, selling his products wherever he could.

By complete coincidence he accidentally cross-bred two types of onions – a Ptuj lük, a cultivar native to eastern Slovenia, and an Egyptian red. Thus in 1947 he created the now famous Raka red onion. When Anton Ulčnik realized he had grown an unbelievably tasty and fertile onion that was high in demand, both as fully-grown onions for food and as sets for planting, he decided to increase his production and sales. His network of interested parties expanded, and soon 1.5 acres of land was no longer sufficient, and in 1965 he rented a further 3.5 acres from a neighboring abandoned farm, and, as the "Father" of the Raka onion, soon also became its biggest producer.

At the same time he also gradually abandoned his shoe making business, far too preoccupied with his new onion. It had become his life, his driving force. His children say that he never really liked being a cobbler, but persisted as it put food on the table. Later work on the farm became much easier when his neighbor acquired a tractor and Anton paid him to till his fields.

To start with they also planted other vegetables beside the onions (carrots, turnips, beats, and corn), which they also sold, often to the nuns in a nearby convent. Later, however, they focused solely on the onion. The children remember good harvests and bad harvests – everything depended on Mother Nature. Their son Franci, who stayed on the farm, remembers that in 1975 they harvested as much as 50 tons of onions. Their biggest customer was the Celje-based company Agro Promet, and they also sold plenty more locally to industries whose canteens made lunch for thousands of workers a day. The Jutranjka textile factory, where the younger Amalija and Ida would one day work, was also a regular customer. Anton abandoned his large-scale onion farming operation after the death of his wife on 15 August

1978, and from then produced only onion sets, right until his death on 23 August 1992.

Anton and Amalija Ulčnik's firstborn was a son, Melania's oldest uncle, born 12 October 1935, and was named after his father with the addition of the name Željko. He began elementary school in Judendorf-Strassengel, and completed it in Raka in the early 1950s. Towards the end of elementary school his grades were far from stable, from Cs up to Bs and back down to Ds. His behavior was good, but he struggled with History and Science for a while. Teachers also said he came to school irregularly, that he always had his head in the clouds, while they noted his parents were extremely sensitive about their little boy, a trait that runs in the family, showing that the Ulčniks looked after their many children.

The third child (the second child was named Ida but she died shortly after birth) Stanislav, or Stanko for short, was born on 3 August 1938 and just like Anton started school while still in exile, continuing in Raka upon their return. Things went well for the first 4 years, though his grades dropped from Bs to Cs in his 4th year. He had top marks for his behavior and singing and Cs and Ds in other subjects. He did the worst in his Slovenian class, which is understandable, as all his previous schooling in Judendorf-Strassengel had been in German, though his teachers always considered him a "tidy and regular student," with only 3 excused and 3 unexcused absences. The schoolteachers gave positive reviews of his parents, saying that they "looked well after their children" and were very "sensitive to their needs." They also noted that Stanko lived in appropriate conditions, sharing a bedroom with his brother Anton.

Nothing with Stanko indicated anything catastrophic, nevertheless everything seems to have fallen apart in 5th grade, starting with a fail in Geography, followed by a whole series of other terrible grades. A complete failure followed in the second semester and he did not even finish the grade, failing History, Geography, and Science. He still had top grades for singing and music, and good marks for behavior too. The poor young man had to repeat the grade, and finished with mostly C grades (Slovenian, Serbo-Croatian, Russian, History, Geography, Science, Mathematics), a B in Drawing and top marks for Singing, Physical Education, and behavior. He kept up the good work into the next school year, 1951/1952. Apparently his crisis from the previous year had been successfully resolved.

Melania Trump's oldest aunt, Ida Ulčnik, had unbelievably varied results throughout her then seven compulsory years of elementary school, getting Ds in 1945/1946, but straight As the next year. She passed the following two years with Bs, followed by a disastrous year with fails in Slovenian, Serbo-Croatian, and Calculus & Geometry. She clearly had to retake her exams in the autumn and then went on to successfully complete her last two years of elementary school. Despite her inconsistent grades, she was praised by her teachers as hardworking, clean, tidy, and with excellent behavior, though they did note that in the 1946/1947 school year she missed class twice for not having shoes and twice because she was working in the fields. Probably a sign of the serious shortages in food and goods in Yugoslavia and

Slovenia immediately after the war, but also a literal confirmation of the proverb that *"the shoemaker's children go barefoot."*

Melanija's aunt, Olga Ulčnik, born 30 October 1943 in Judendorf-Strassengel, flourished at school. She averaged excellent grades from 1950 to 1954, even finishing the last year with straight As except for one B in Calculus & Geometry. Olga's personality was also lauded by her teachers, who called her "calm and serious," a student who "looked after care of school supplies, was reliable, hard-working, and very fair to schoolmates." She was even discussed twice at meetings of the teachers' council, stressing that she was the best student in her class, and that she should be send to further her education in Celje. This was arranged and in 1956 Olga went to Celje, the third-largest town in Slovenia, some 45 miles from Raka. The state was obliged to provide her room and board. Without question, Olga being sent to school in Celje, a town also known for its medieval counts, was a huge achievement and an honor for Olga and her family and the social recognition that she really was very a good, talented, and prospective young student, was so much more important in a communist state, where the individual was only as good as the totalitarian authorities acknowledged.

Melanija's mother Amalija, the sixth child of Anton and Amalija Ulčnik, started elementary school in Raka in the year the duration of elementary education was changed from seven to eight years. She started on 1 September 1952 at the age of seven, up until recently, normal practice in Slovenia. Amalija did well, getting Bs throughout her schooling, only slipping to Cs in 7th grade. Her behavior was excellent throughout. In her final semester, the mother of the future Melania Trump and the future grandmother of Barron William Trump received the following grades: As in Slovenian, Art, Singing and Physical Education; Bs in Serbo-Croatian, German, Geography, Science, Physics and Chemistry; Cs in Calculus & Geometry and History. She had also had top marks in handwork which included needlework, offered between 3rd and 5th grades, and indeed she went on to become a seamstress.

Through all eight years of school Amalija Ulčnik only had two unexcused hours, with thirty-three excused hours. Her teachers thought very highly of her, saying interestingly, *"Extremely tidy, well-behaved, good with her classmates, fairly quick thinking, very sensitive, emotional, more mentally than physically developed, active in class, assertive, with an exceptional knack for imagination."* About her parents they wrote that they *"are very interested in her progress and are raising her well!"*

Anton and Amalija's next child, Marija, born in Raka on 18 October 1949, entered first grade in September of 1956. For her first three years she was an excellent student, slacking a bit in 4th grade, but then finishing the next three years successfully, ultimately ending elementary school with a B average. Her behavior was excellent throughout, and she never received a grade lower than a B, finishing her elementary schooling in June 1964. Marija too was praised by her teachers, who remarked, *"dependable, tidy, honest, persistent, a good classmate, eager to help those who need it, well-adjusted and sociable, diligent and precise, physically and mentally well-developed, follows lessons without problems, perhaps a bit lazy and too chatty sometimes, but quick to grasp new concepts, with a good memory and well-kept notebooks, exhibits a range of emotions and responds well to praise, sometimes a little conceited, likes to be the center of attention, but has a good relationship with teachers."* Her parents were also singled out for praise, reportedly, *"taking great interest in her progress, providing an excellent upbringing for Marija at home and providing good living conditions."* The only afterthought was provided by the homeroom teacher, who remarked that *"she has a lot of work at home, and she could do even better in school if she didn't have as much."*

Franci, the Ulčniks' last child, was born in Raka on 12 April 1952 and started school in September 1959. He was an A student throughout, "only" earning a B average in 8th grade and a single C in Chemistry towards the end of his schooling. His finished his elementary schooling in June 1967, just 3 years before the birth of Melanija Knavs. Franci's exceptional academic performance was also reflected in similar evaluations of his behavior, with the teachers positively gushing over him and his parents: *"Suitably developed physically and mentally, the most scholastically advanced of the boys, one of the most gifted and hard-working, which is the result of a great upbringing at home, tidy and honest, serious, reliable, school supplies are always neat and in order, has exemplary writing, regularly does his homework, is open-minded, persistent, well-behaved, has no problem understanding course work, has a great memory and active imagination, is interested in everything and asks tons of questions, comes to conclusions well, undertakes to earn the highest possible grade, is a good classmate and likes to help other children, is very popular, has a positive effect on the class and still earns the respect of his schoolmates, but he is lively and a bit of a clown, in his spare time something of a humorist, entertaining the whole class, he is emotional and respects his parents and teachers, and is an extremely independent child."* They added that, *"when not studying, he looks after children, or is out cutting firewood, or something similar. His parents don't let him just lounge around and are always interested in how he is doing at school."* Finally they remarked that, *"conditions are good at home, the boy is always well-dressed and has appropriate school supplies."*

The Ulčnik daughters, Melania's mother Amalija and aunt Ida, continued their schooling together and even their careers at the same socialist factory – Jutranjka. And still today, Ida is the one taking care of their home and garden in Sevnica, while Amalija and Viktor Knavs are in United States. With their father a cobbler, and mother trained seamstress, it comes as no surprise that the girls decided to take up the craft as well, also becoming seamstresses after finishing elementary school. Ida more or less set the path for her six-year younger sister Amalija, who followed Ida every step through trade school and later to Jutranjka, where both women ended up working until their retirement.

The vocational school in Celje, which took on metal and textile apprentices, had a long tradition in the town, as it was founded when during Austro-Hungarian rule in 1883. A few years after the end of the Second World War, the communist regime renamed the school in honor of Boris Kidrič – the country's first communist president after the war. The school had a noble goal, which it fulfilled admirably, that was to take on apprentices from the countryside, which lacked vocational schools. Those attending the school came from all over rural Slovenia, so the school needed to provide accommodation and food, though not all the students took advantage of this. The three-year program also included work experience so the students attended class all year round but only had classes a few days per week.

Ida enrolled in this vocational school in the 1955 / 1956 school year, earning Bs throughout. At the same time she also worked at the state socialist female tailoring salon, Moda in Celje. As expected, there were only girls in her class, around fifteen on average. She missed class very rarely, not once in her second year, and not once was her absence unexcused. In her final year Ida earned three As, specifically in Accounting, Industrial Sketching, and behavior, with four Bs in Slovenian, Law and the Economy of the Socialist Federal Republic of Yugoslavia, Physical Education, and Technology.

Her homeroom teacher Bogomil Spačapan evaluated her in 1956 / 1957 as *"quiet, mostly introverted, hard-working and bright,"* and since she displayed exceptional knowledge at the end of her second year, they awarded her with a book, but, as her teacher added, she had *"little sense of collective,"* which was not really ideal in a communist state.

During her three years there, before earning her diploma in June 1958, Ida moved 3 times. Her address in her third year was Bohoričeva Street number 4, which is right under Celje Hill, where the famous church and monastery of St. Joseph are located. The homeroom teacher Spačapan gave a final, in those days it was called 'moral', evaluation of Ida, highlighting her uncooperativeness and the fact that she was the quietest girl in her class, who *"withdraws from the influence of the collective, which doesn't care much for her, even though she is a faithful and bright student."* This led the teacher to wonder whether the old saying that still waters run deep held true for Ida.

Ida Ulčnik headed off to Maribor after finishing vocational school to enroll in another three-year program for highly qualified workers, earning her degree on 24 June 1962. This brought her six-year education as a seamstress to a close, after which she had the expertise to find a full-time job at the Jutranjka factory in Sevnica.

Melania Trump's mother Amalija entered the Boris Kidrič vocational school in 1960, at the age of fifteen, five years after her sister Ida had matriculated. The program suited her perfectly, and she was primarily a straight-A student, especially her first year where she had all As in Slovenian, Home Economics, Accounting, Hygiene, Physical Education, Industrial Sketching, and Practical Work. Unsurprisingly, she also had top marks for behavior.

In a class of eighteen girls, Amalija soon emerged as the leader, even being elected class president, a testament to her popularity. She had the same homeroom teacher as her sister had had, Bogomil Spačapan, who considered her a *"wonderful worker in the school's workshop, with a passion for sewing and a commitment to hard work."* In her second year Amalija "only" got six As, including in behavior, and three Bs, which rightfully led Spačapan to remark that she had *"slacked a little bit,"* but he still wrote highly of her at the end of the year, saying she was *"relaxed, polite, respectful, bright, hard-working, and a promising seamstress who loves her job."*

During her schooling, Amalija Ulčnik lived in Celje where she rented modest rooms. Amalija never had an unexcused absence, and before leaving to work in the Sevnica-based children's clothing factory Jutranjka, she worked in Celje's state clothing company Elegant.

As with the vocational school in Celje, it was Amalija's sister Ida who led the way to the Jutranjka factory, landing a full-time job as a seamstress' assistant in the company's first year of business, starting on 1 October 1962. She was twenty-three at the time and worked there until her retirement in 1990.

Amalija, who would six years later become Melanija's proud mother, followed her sister to Jutranjka fifteen months later, on 15 March 1964. She was nineteen at the time and, just like Ida, worked at Jutranjka until her retirement in 1997.

Both the Ulčnik sisters were employed at Jutranjka as highly qualified seamstresses, but their roles in production were vastly different from one another. Ida was promoted from her first job as assistant seamstress to head of exports, then worked in quality control, ultimately becoming head of the whole factory's quality control department, a clearly successful communist worker's career.

Her younger sister Amalija, who now lives on New York's prestigious Fifth Avenue, never sought a higher education. As a result her career remained more stagnant and she worked as a pattern constructor until 1973 when the company was split into smaller units to comply with new legislation. Amalija Ulčnik was placed in the so-called Basic Organization of Associated Labor called Motiv.

The Jutranjka company, which had its production line located in a Salesian monastery that was expropriated after the war, was founded by the Municipality of Sevnica in February 1962, and entered into the registry of companies in July of the same year. It specialized in children's clothes and swimwear. It was, of course, a socialist company under state ownership, as it was impossible to found private businesses in communist Yugoslavia, apart from small private trades, employing at most seven people, and private farms working a limited amount of land.

Like other socialist companies of the day, Jutranjka did not have proper owners, but was run by the workers' council through operative directors. The state itself attempted to replace the role of the non-existent owners through state ministries, institutions, municipalities, and through communist cells both within and outside the company.

In December 1966 Jutranjka's workers' council renamed the company to reflect its focus on children's clothes into Factory of Children's Clothing Jutranjka, with another tweak to the name in 1970 when it was changed to Children's Clothing Industry Jutranjka. In 1973 new complicated economic legislature was introduced, forcing the company to reorganize into several smaller basic labor organizations.

To the public, Jutranjka, the Yugoslavian and Slovenian company that played such an important role in the future Melania Trump's life, remained a single factory, but internally it was reorganized into several administratively separate working units with their own supervision and leadership. This destructive division, enacted into law throughout communist Yugoslavia, had the ideological purpose of bringing management directly into the hands of the manufacturers or the proletariat, and from the early seventies Yugoslavia began developing its unique worker self-management. The theoretical father of this beautiful but useless and in practice destructive utopian ideal was the Slovenian Edvard Kardelj, second only to Tito in the Yugoslavian communist leadership. He was, just like the first communist president of Slovenia Boris Kidrič, responsible for the deaths of many political enemies on Slovenian territory after the war. The obligatory introduction of self-management, due to its socialistic way of management, dealt a huge blow to the already inefficient economic management of the country and contributed to the even more rapid decline of Communism in Yugoslavia.

When Jutranjka was broken apart into five basic labor organizations, Amalija ended up at Motiv, where 240 of the company's 1038 employees were relocated. Given that the company was only 11 years old at the time, and had started with only 39 employees, this was certainly considered rapid company growth.

Though, as one might expect in a textile factory, the work force was overwhelmingly female, the job descriptions in the list of tasks were always male. This was also true of the post of "konstruktor," or pattern maker, which was filled predominantly by women, among them Melanija's mom Amalija. For example, at the end of 1978 there were seven female and one male pattern makers at the Motiv unit and in the Modelarna unit where Amalija was working by then ten female and one male pattern workers.

As a pattern maker, a kind of intermediary between a designer and a seamstress, Amalija was responsible for creating the patterns for mass production and monitoring how a given pattern affected the final product. They worked with designers and used the designers' sketches to create the pattern, which they then drew by hand, and later by computer. The pattern maker would mark the fabric to be sewn, scrutinize the working model, make corrections, shorten, lengthen, or otherwise tailor the pattern, then approve it, and ultimately produce it in several sizes. After that the pattern maker would then monitor the whole production process from sketch, to cutting and sewing, all the way up till the whole run was finished. The pattern maker was also responsible for picking the right fabric for a design, taking into consideration its texture, any printed patterns, as well as accessories, and also needed to keep abreast of trends and requirements in the textile market.

American journalist Charlotte Hays erroneously elevated Amalija Knavs' pattern making position to "fashion designer," and the socialist company Jutranjka became "fashion industry," in her book *The Fortune Hunters*, written in 2007.

On 29 July 1967, Amalija Ulčnik married Viktor Knavs, then personal driver for officials at the municipality of Trbovlje. Their wedding, to which only their closest friends and family were invited, was held at City Hall in Ljubljana, but the reception afterwards was organized slightly north of the capital, at the even today still highly prestigious Podvin Castle. That the young lovebirds married so far away from their hometowns was something extremely rare in Slovenian in those days, probably points to the fact that Amalija and Viktor are were not particularly attached to their roots. Amalija's witness was her eldest brother, Anton Željko, and Viktor's best man was his brother, Herman.

The newlyweds headed off toward Podvin Castle in a Ford Taunus, driven by the late Matjaž Han Sr., father of Matjaž Han Jr., who is a very well-known politician in Slovenia, a Member of Parliament for the Social Democrats, the party of the former Communists, a businessman, and former mayor of the Municipality of Radeče.

The Han and Knavs families were very close, spending their traditional annual summer vacation together in Novalja on the Croatian island of Pag. Matjaž Han Jr. remembers that Viktor Knavs' best man at his wedding to Amalija was his father, and not Viktor's brother Herman.

Their civil union was followed on 3 October 1967 with a church service in the bride's hometown, at the Church of St. Lawrence in Raka. Viktor made a bit of a political gamble in getting married in a church, as he was a member of the Communist Party. He was not a senior-ranked member, but marrying in a religious ceremony was a no-go at the time. He could easily have been accused of being in serious violation of party rules and thrown out, not bidding well for furthering his career.

Forty-eight years later, on 30 October 2015, journalists from the British tabloid the *Daily Mail* wrongly reported on their website in a long piece about the potential future First Lady Melania Trump, that her parents Viktor Knavs and Amalija Ulčnik never married in a church.

The editors at the *Daily Mail* made a huge mistake in their research; they otherwise correctly reported that Viktor Knavs was a member or the Yugoslavian and Slovenian Communist Party, but they submitted as proof a party document from the Archives of the Republic of Slovenia, where they had tracked down a wrong Viktor. They even got his birthday wrong, saying he was born on 24 March 1947, instead of the correct date of 23 November 1941. Written proof that Viktor Knavs was truly a member of the Communist Party can be obtained from membership records from 1987. The authentic records were first published in the first edition of *Melania Trump: The Inside Story* on Amazon. What is particularly interesting about Viktor Knavs being a member of the Community Party, is the fact that he never officially resigned from it. Clear records exist of those who left the party and Melania Trump's or Melanija Knavs' father is not among them. Viktor Knavs only stopped being a member of the Slovenian and Yugoslavian Communist Party on the day the party was politically and physically dissolved.

Trump's campaign team initially officially denied Viktor Knavs' membership of the Communist Party. Most likely because it was one of those things that the Knavs family had kept hidden from Donald Trump.

It was probably Fif and Malči's (as friends affectionately called Viktor and Amalija) wedding that instigated Viktor leaving his job at the municipality on 3 April 1968, eight months after the nuptials, to take on the position of driver for the director of Jutranjka. He held this post for about a year until he was dismissed on 15 May 1969, for the lack of work ethic.

Viktor had a reputation for not taking well to authority, not exactly a character trait that bodes well for someone working as a personal chauffeur to an important director or mayor. He was also not the only person fired from Jutranjka in 1969, as two women were dismissed for suspected theft.

Even though Viktor was literally thrown out of Jutranjka, it is interesting to note that this did not seem to affect the company's socialist policy toward the family regarding the apartment they lived in. At the time their address was a state-owned one-bedroom apartment in Sevnica, in the Naselje Heroja Maroka housing development number 7, given to them by Jutranjka. In the early 1970s, after the birth of their second daughter Melanija, Jutranjka also gave them a bigger apartment in the same housing development.

On 4 May 1980 the long-time communist dictator of Yugoslavia, Josip Broz Tito, died in Ljubljana after a prolonged and difficult illness. With his death the regime triggered quite a hysteria of mourning throughout the country. Grown adults cried in the streets, at their jobs, at institutions, and children wept in schools. Teary-eyed people stood in line everywhere to write their condolences into mourning books set up around the country. People who had had their lives or the lives of friends and family ruined by the regime, silently stood back, as it was extremely dangerous to say anything critical of the late communist Yugoslav leader during this mourning frenzy.

On Monday, 5 May, the coffin with Tito's remains was loaded onto his blue train, which set off from Ljubljana on the 300-mile journey to Belgrade. Several million Yugoslavians lined the railroad tracks to silently say goodbye to their beloved leader. When the train passed through Sevnica, where the Knavs family was living, just as elsewhere in the country, the entire town gathered along the railroad crossing. As befitting, the factory Jutranjka too, immediately started its own book of condolences, and all the workers signed it, including Ida and Amalija. The first page of the book featured a picture of the late dictator in its upper right-hand corner, with a diagonal black line across the corner of the page, indicating the book's purpose. Tito's death date was calligraphically written in the upper left corner, with a verse adapted from a poem by the Slovenian poet Mila Kačič: *It is not life that binds us, nor death that separates us – the bonds are stronger (Ni življenje tisto, ki nas veže, in smrt ni tisto, ki ločuje nas – so vezi močnejše).* At the bottom of the page gleamed a large five-pointed star, one of the most important symbols of the Yugoslavian Communists.

Ten years before the death of Tito, specifically on 26 April 1970, at the maternity ward in a hospital in Novo Mesto Melanija Knavs cried her first tears. It was a warm, windy and slightly rainy day. Her mother Amalija and father Viktor probably never though about how the name they had chosen for their newborn daughter, Melanija, is a version of the originally Greek name Melania, which would become Melanija's official name some 25 years later.

The Ulčnik and Knavs Family Tree

Željko Anton Ulčnik
- 2. 10. 1935 (Raka)

Ida Ulčnik
- 1936 (Raka)
- Died shortly after birth

Elizabeta Ulčnik
- 9. 11. 1906 (Koble)

Stanislav Ulčnik
- 3. 8. 1938 (Raka)

Anton Ulčnik
- Cca. 1880 (Koble)

Šimon Ulčnik
- 28. 11. 1908 (Podob)

Ida Ulčnik
- 11. 9. 1939 (Raka)

Anton Ulčnik
- 9. 1. 1910 (Podob)
- 29. 8. 1992 (Raka)

Olga Ulčnik
- 30. 10. 1943 (Judendorf-Strassengel)

MARRIAGE:
Sv. Jernej pri Ločah

MARRIAGE:
(Raka)

Amalija Ulčnik
- 9. 7. 1945 (Judendorf-Strassengel)

Ines Knavs (Ines Knauss)
- 9. 1. 1968 (Novo mesto)

MARRIAGE:
3. 10. 1967 (Raka)
29. 7. 1967
(Ljubljana Cityhall)

Marjeta Petelinc
- Cca. 1885 (Brezje)

Amalija Gliha
- 9. 4. 1913
- 15. 8. 1978 (Raka)

Marjeta Ulčnik
- 21. 5. 1914 (Podob)

Viktor Knavs (Waldemar Knaus)
- 23. 11. 1941 (Jagnjenica)

Melanija Knavs (Melania Knauss)
- 26. 4. 1970 (Novo mesto)

Mija Ulčnik (Marica)
- 18. 10. 1949 (Raka)

Franc Ulčnik
- 12. 4. 1952 (Raka)

- BIRTH
- DEATH
- MARRIAGE

Anton Knavs
✪ 8. 6. 1899

Anton Knavs
✪ 10. 6. 1874
(Jelovo)

Frančiška Knavs
✪ 19. 8. 1901

Joško Knavs
✪ 1932 (Jagnjenica)
❶ 4. 7. 1940 (Jagnjenica)

☺ MARRIAGE:
7. 11. 1898
(Jelovo)

Jožef Knavs
✪ 3. 3. 1904
(Jelovo)
❶ 10. 1. 1989
(Radeče)

Viktor Knavs
(Waldemar Knaus)
✪ 23. 11. 1941
(Jagnjenica)

Ines Knavs
(Ines Knauss)
✪ 9. 1. 1968
(Novo mesto)

Alojzija Bevk
✪ 13. 5. 1877
(Sv. Jurij)

☺ MARRIAGE:
6. 9. 1931
(Jelovo)

☺ MARRIAGE:
3. 10. 1967
(Raka)
29. 7. 1967
(Ljubljana
Cityhall)

Antonija Ribič
✪ 1907
(Mrtovec)
❶ 27. 4. 1973
(Radeče)

Franc Knavs
✪ 22. 6. 1906

Amalija Ulčnik
✪ 9. 7. 1945
(Judendorf-
Strassengel)

Melanija Knavs
(Melania Knauss)
✪ 26. 4. 1970
(Novo mesto)

Amalija Knavs
✪ 24. 3. 1909

Marija Knavs
✪ 31. 3. 1911

Herman Knavs
(Hermann Knaus)
✪ 17. 4. 1944
(Radeče)

Julijana Knavs
✪ 5. 2. 1913

Kristina Knavs
✪ 15. 7. 1914

Štev.
Num.

KRSTNI LIST - Testimonium baptismi

Iz krstne župnije
Extractus e libro baptizatorum parochiae   **SEVNICA**

Zvezek   **1968**   stran   **25**   številka   -

Tomus   pagina   numerus

Datum, kraj, župnija rojstva Dies, locus, parochia nativitatis	26. april 1970 – Novo Mesto	
Datum krsta Dies baptismi	14. junij 1970 – Raka	
I m e nomen	**Melanija**	
Zakonski, nezak., civilno zakon. Sin, hči Legitimus, illeg. civ. leg. filius, filia	zak. hči	
priimek, ime, poklic, vera, očeta	Knavs Viktor, šofer r.k.v.	oče rojen 23. 11. 1941
cognomen, nomen, cond. religio patris		
priimek, ime, poklic, vera matere	Amalija Ulčnik, Šivilja, r.k.v.	9.7. 1945
cognomen, nomen cond. rel. matris		
poročena /copulati	3. oktober 1967 – Raka	
kraj, št. župnija bivališča staršev Locus, num. parochia commorationis	NHM 9, Sevnica	
Priimek, ime, poklic botrov Cognomen, nomen, cond. patrinorum	Ulčnik Ida, šivilja, NHM 16	
Krstitelj / baptizans	Čampa Franc – župnik	
Opomba (pozakonitev, birma, poroka) Adnotatio (legitim., confirm., matrimon.,		

Župnija Sevnica,   dne 5. 11. 2015
Ex officio parochiali

Vinko Štrucelj – župnik

Melanija Knavs' birth certificate (authors' documentation).

IZ NOVOMEŠKE PORODNIŠNICE

Pretekli teden so v novomeški porodnišnici rodile: **Majda Rudman** z Vrha pri Ljubnu — Darka, **Milica Tancik** iz Metlike — Bena, **Marija Penič** iz Bereče vasi — Silvo, **Zlata Brezinšek** iz Senuš — Marijo, **Valerija Mirt** z Velikega Trna — Alenko, **Antonija Andoljšek** iz Regerče vasi — Renato, **Cvetka Dragoš** iz Cerkvišča — Vesno, **Barica Slanac** iz Bratovanjcev — Branka, **Amalija Knavs** iz Sevnice — Melanijo, **Tatjana Petelin** iz Uršnih sel — Liljano, **Stanka Bobnar** iz Petan — Igorja, **Anica Vrhovšek** iz Drnovega — Roberta, **Terezija Pucelj** iz Žužemberka — Franca, **Jožefa Staniša** iz Gotne vasi — deklico, **Neža Dulc** iz Stranja — dečka, **Ana Mesojedec** iz Češče vasi — 2 deklici, **Ana Kozole** s Senovega — deklico, **Katarina Zupanič** iz Črnomlja — deklico, **Fanika Novak** s Senovega — deklico, **Barbara Železnjak** iz Loke — deklico, **Ana Weiss** iz Radovlje — deklico in **Ana Kobe** iz Ločne — deklico. — Čestitamo!

Announcement in local newspaper on the birth of Melania Knavs (*Dolenjski List*, 7 May 1970, section on News from the Novo Mesto Maternity Ward).

Jelovo – Family home of Melanija's paternal great-grandfather (authors' documentation).

Jagnjenica – the village Melanja's father Viktor Knavs was born in (Jože Potrpin, Skriti zaklad: Kronika Župnije Svibno, 2002 – Celje Central Library).

Judendorf-Strassengel – Town in Austria where Melanija's mother Amalija Ulčnik was born (authors' documentation).

Raka – Hometown of Melanija's mother Amalija Ulčnik (authors' documentation).

Sevnica during the years of Melanija's youth (authors' documentation).

The Jutranjka socialist textile factory (Zbornik Jutranjka, 1962-1982, Večer, 1982 – Celje Central Library).

Amalija's workplace at the factory (Zbornik Jutranjka, 1962-1982 - Celje Central Library).

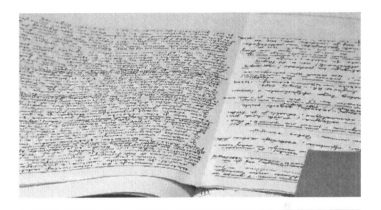

Melanija's elementary school report card, shown to Pop TV by Sevnica Elementary School's principal Mirjana Jelančič.

Melanija's father Viktor Knavs - member of Yugoslav Communist Party (The Archives of the Republic of Slovenia).

Summer 1988 - Melanija in the fashion magazine *Maneken* (photo: Vito Komac, *Maneken*, Slovenian edition, 1988).

Fall-winter 1988 - Melanija in the fashion magazine *Maneken* (*Maneken*, Slovenian edition, 1988/1989).

Melanija at a spring/summer fashion show 1992/1993 (*Naša Žena*, February 1993).

Melanija – Finalists for 1992 Look of the Year (all photos: Dean Dubokovič, Lady, August 2002; Jana, January 1999).

Look of the Year 1992 – Third-placed Melanija with Stojan Auer (photo: Dean Dubokovič, Lady, August 2002).

Sevnica – Melanija's apartment until she left for Ljubljana (authors' documentation).

Ljubljana – Melanija's apartment until she left to go abroad (authors' documentation).

Melanija on Studio City playing Melanija – The President of the United States of America (Obrazi, August 2006).

REPORTAŽE, ZANIMIVOSTI

Donald Trump na slovenski zabavi

Dan slovenske samostojnosti so proslavili tudi onkraj Velike luže - slovensko veleposlaništvo v Washingtonu je v elitnem hotelu Plaza pripravilo sprejem za številne Slovence, ki živijo v Združenih državah, Američane in tuje diplomate. Gostitelja, **dr. Davorin Kračun** in njegova soproga **Andreja**, sta v Plazo povabila tudi eno najslavnejših slovenskih manekenk **Melanijo Knavs**, ki je že pred leti bliskovito uspela v tujini, nato pa je svetovni rumeni tisk polnila predvsem z ljubezensko afero z ameriškim milijonarjem. Ko je vstopila dolgonoga lepotica, je med gosti je presenečeno završalo - bolj kot nma pa je tokrat poglede pritegnil njen spremljevalec, ki je bil nihče drug kot veliki **Donald Trump**. V sproščenem klepetu s Kračunovima je pohvalil (očrno še vedno) svojo Melanijo kot veliko ambasadorko Slovenije.   (sdr)

Donald Trump in Melanija Knavs na sprejemu pri Kračunovih

Melanija with Slovenian journalists in Paris 1998 (Dušan Nograšek, *Nedeljski Dnevnik*, September 1998).

Newspaper article in *Večer* about Donald Trump attending a party to mark the anniversary of Slovenian independence; in the photo Donald Trump, Melania Knauss with Davorin and Andreja Kračun (published 19 January 2001)

Chapter 3

THE KNAVS SISTERS

The date of the future Melania Trump's birth almost co-incided with a big state anniversary that the Communists in Slovenia celebrated solemnly. 27 April 1941 marked the founding of the Liberation Front of the Slovene Nation as a broad political association against the German, Italian, and Hungarian occupiers during the Second World War. In truth the Front was not originally directed toward the invaders, as it was made up of Slovenian Communists, led from Moscow, and only later were the various political groups subordinated by the front, achieving through it the Communist takeover. When the Front was first founded the Communists were theoretically still Hitler's allies as a result of the German-Soviet Pact. Only after the unannounced Nazi attack on Stalin on 22 June 1941 did the Slovenian Communists begin their resistance against the Nazi occupiers in Slovenia.

Melanija was the second and last Knavs child, with Amalija and Viktor's first daughter Ines having been born two years earlier, in January 1968, just five months after their wedding. Both Melanija and Ines were born in Novo Mesto, the regional center of southeastern Slovenia. The hospital is a little less than an hour's drive away from Sevnica, where the Knavses lived.

It may seem strange that Amalija and Viktor did not choose the maternity ward in Brežice, a much closer town on the border with Croatia, but it is true that the hospital in Novo Mesto had a much better reputation. Brežice's bad reputation meant concerned expectant mothers preferred to go and give birth further away from home rather than risk any complications.

Both Ines' and Melanija's births were reported in the local newspaper, the still widely read *Dolenjski List*. Under the section 'From the Novo Mesto Maternity Ward' the 11 January 1968 issue *"Amalija Knavs from Sevnica – Ines,"* and the 7 May 1970 issue says *"Amalija Knavs from Sevnica – Melanija."* The delay between the birth of the Knavs girls and the newspaper report is a result of the editors of *Dolenjski List* only getting the good news once the happy mothers left the hospital with their babies.

Both Ines and Melanija were baptized in Raka, their mother's hometown, in the church of St. Lawrence. Ines was baptized on 4 February 1968, about a month after her birth, while Melanija's christening came on 14 June 1970, around 2 months after she was born. The master of ceremonies was pastor Franc Čampa, and Melanija's godmother was her mother's sister, Ida Ulčnik.

Once more, the *Daily Mail* made incorrect reports about this matter, saying that Melanija was never christened and that had never received communion. As he had done with his own wedding, Viktor Knavs, a member of the Slovenian Communist Party, took a big risk in baptizing his daughters, as the party's atheist leaders would not have tolerated any religious behavior. Only an atheist could be a member of the Communist Party, someone who did not believe in any god, and religious rituals of any kind were strictly prohibited in the families of obedient communists. In practice though, many, often well-known and politically active communists in Slovenia regularly broke the rule, always in secret, of course. Many documents in the archives of the Slovenian State Security Administration, the secret political police known for short by the original acronym for the Yugoslav State Security Administration UDBA, there are numerous documents showing how individuals breaking this prohibition were reported by UDBA to the Communist authorities.

Sisters Ines and Melanija Knavs grew up in the small town of Sevnica with, then as now, around 5,000 inhabitants. Sevnica is an important local hub, as its textile and woodworking factories employ many people from the immediate and extended surroundings. The town sits on the east bank of the Sava River, and the railroad dating back to 1862 runs through it. The historic town center preserves several old buildings, including the churches of St. Nicholas and St. Florian from the 14th century, all attesting to Sevnica's long history and tradition. An imposing castle, which can be dated to the first half of the 12th century, can be found on the hill rising above the town. The area suffered a similar fate during the Second World War to the other places associated with Melanija's parents with, Hitler's troops forcibly removing many locals, some of which never returned from exile and the labor camps.

Though Melania Trump is unarguably the best known and wealthiest person ever to come from Sevnica, the town can also boast several other famous or successful people; the painter Nina Bedek, the cultural worker Albert Felicijan, after whom a great hall in Sevnica castle is named, the former CEO of Petrol and Avtotehna (the country's largest fuel provider and one of its largest car dealers and servicers) Boris Perko, the Slovenian composer Jakob Jež, the well-known electrical engineer Jurij F. Tasić, the rapper Naske Mehić, who pocketed €92,000 after winning the Slovenian version of Big Brother in 2008, a record sum for Slovenian reality shows, and the beautiful model and Miss Slovenia Nataša Pinoza. We could also include Sebastian or Matjaž Gornik in this list of well-known people hailing from Sevnica, though he is famous for his notoriety. Gornik was condemned on multiple occasions of robbery and arson, but the locals know him as the artist and writer who, at the age of just fifteen, got into a strange scandal with Damjan Murko, a celebrity from Maribor, when, according to the media, Gornik stole Murko's identity.

The newlywed Knavses had received a one-bedroom apartment in a five-story building from Jutranjka in 1967 at the address Naselje Heroja Maroka 9, and three years after Melanija's birth they were given a three-bedroom apartment in a newly-built building on the same street, number 27, just a few yards from their old home. In front of their first home was a row of free-standing garages, in one of which Viktor kept his obligatory Mercedes and various other odds and ends.

The Naselje Heroja Maroka housing development was named after the national hero Alojz Kolman with the nom-de-guerre 'Marok', born in the village of Zabukovje about Sevnica, a member of the partisan resistance movement who was killed during the war. The neighborhood lies at the center of Sevnica, on a slight elevation, and has a hodge-podge of apartment buildings of varying shapes, sizes, and years of construction. The largest building, however, is only five stories high, which doesn't hold a candle to Trump Tower in New York, where Amalija, Viktor, and until recently Ines Knavs, live today. It is a typical socialist neighborhood, built in stages in Tito's Yugoslavia from 1960 to 1976. There are several grassy areas and parks, giving the neighborhood a warm and friendly feeling despite the dull and uniform buildings. From the broad sidewalks winding through the grassy areas surrounding the apartment blocks the hubbub of downtown cannot be heard, despite being just a short walk away. All around the apartment buildings there are children playing, in the same place that Melania played thirty-five years ago, and plenty young mothers pushing strollers, and residents taking their dogs out for a walk.

Today most of the surrounding buildings have been renovated, painted in bright colors, and there are numerous new cars parked outside. There are several garages, as well, but there is nowhere near enough space for all the cars, as statistics show a rapid increase in the number of cars per capita in Slovenia. When the apartments were built having a vehicle of any sort was a rare treasure and far too few parking spaces were planned for today's standards.

Melanija's childhood living in Sevnica was nothing special, no different to the thousands of other Slovenian girls, though it is true that she was pretty even then. She was a sweet and gentle girl, a bit teasing at times. Melanija never felt embarrassed, accepted how she was, and always had an air of self-confident, during photographic sessions for fashion magazines, where she appeared as a child model. The legendary fashion photographer Stane Jerko, who 'discovered' Melanija just before her 17th birthday, said that she was shy and tense at their first session, though we can imagine that the postpubescent young Melanija found it a bit more challenging to pose for a famous Ljubljana professional photographer which was quite different to what she had been used to in the playful and relaxed sessions for children's fashion magazines in her domestic environment.

Other children used to call Melanija "Mali" for short, as the longer form was too complicated for them. This is a double entendre in Slovenian, as *"mali"* means "the little one." But Melanija never let this teasing get to her, since, as she later disclosed, she knew already back then what she wanted to do. She had already found her joy and passion in her youth, which only strengthened her confidence and ambition.

Melanija had always paid attention to her appearance, and she credits her mother Amalija for giving her a skin-care regimen at an early age. She liked anything to do with fashion and beauty and discovered her own talent for design and creation at an early age. In her father's garage, for instance, she cleaned, repaired, and repainted a falling apart old basket and turned it into a plant holder; she was also very fond of knitting.

Melanija's childhood was relatively carefree, as her parents were, in the socialist social scale of things, comfortably middle class, and took very good care of her. She was a calm, smiling and happy girl, sensitive to other people's emotions, though reluctant to display her own. Her influence on her peers was both encouraging, but also calming, as she was never loud or rambunctious. Others found her pleasant to talk to, as well as refined and sophisticated, always saying please and thank you. In short, she was very well brought up.

It was the norm in communism that young children went to daycare, but Ines and Melanija, along with their friend, the few-month older Diana Dernač (today Diana Kosar), downstairs neighbor and daughter of Jože and Ana Dernač, had a different arrangement; a private nanny from the next apartment building, whom they called "auntie," came to look after the three girls every day. Melanija, unable to pronounce the name "Diana," renamed her "Didi," while Diana's mother Ana called Melanija's mother "Malčka" instead of Amalija. Ana Dernač, today a retired accountant, told the Slovenian magazine *Reporter* that Malčka had a good sense for esthetics and even sewed decorations for Diana's crib out of yellow fabric. Later for financial reasons Ana Dernač enrolled her daughter in the state kindergarten, while Ines and Melanija stayed with their private nanny until they went to 1st grade of elementary school, at the ages of six and seven, respectively. Their nanny has sadly passed away, doubtlessly taking with her many interesting anecdotes about the early life of the future Melania Trump.

There were many children growing up in their neighborhood, so the sisters Melanija and Ines always had something going on. The neighborhood children's favorite games were cops and robbers, hide and seek, playing with the then trendy hula hoop, jump rope, setting up shows and competitions, biking, and roller-skating, as well as of course just sitting on the wall outside of building number 9 and chatting the days away. Roller-skating, one of Melanija's favorites, was as popular as inline skating is these days, but it caused a lot of bruised knees, missed lunches, and sometimes even parents angry about torn socks and stockings. Melanija always took to such games calmly, never wanting to stand out or compete if it was not absolutely necessary. She was never one to initiate a game of play outside around the apartment blocks, but was often invited to join in by other children.

"Come, come on, we're outside playing!" they would call her. *"I'll be right there; I just have to read something and I'll join you,"* Melanija usually answered. She also never broke her promise.

Whenever the kids had a fight, Melanija was always the one to diffuse the situation, resolving quite a few crises. In general, Melanija disliked childish fights and grudges, and always tried to sort things out by saying the right thing, being calm and focused and thus ensured that the game always continued.

The kids in the neighborhood also came up with a clever way of communicating with each other, hanging up a woolen string and attaching a note with the clothespins their mothers used to hang out the laundry and pulling on the network of strings to deliver the note to the right window. When the letter reached the sender, they would ring a bell or shake the string to confirm its receipt.

Melanija and her friends, among them Mirjana Jelančič, today the principal of Sevnica Elementary School, mostly played outside, but when one of them had a birthday, they all visited each other, along with their parents. Giant-sized cakes adorned with candles, juice and whipped cream, sundaes and fruit salads, and raspberry nectar from the nearby Dana factory were obligatory at such parties. If they managed to find a bottle of Coca-Cola, it was a real treat, as it was extremely difficult to smuggle this symbol of American capitalism across the Slovenian, or rather Communist Yugoslavian, border in those days.

As she later told the media, Melanija first stepped onto the catwalk in 1975, meaning she was only five at the time. The event was a fashion show in Ljubljana for Slovenia's two textile giants Jutranjka, where her mother worked, and Mura from Murska Sobota. This is hard to verify, as the earliest pictures of Melanija as a model are from January 1977, when the future Mrs. Trump was already almost seven years old. She is pictured along with her friends Diana Kosar and Nena Bedek, whose mother Olga worked with Melanija's mother at Jutranjka. The two had the same position at the factory as pattern makers, and were even neighbors, with Nena Bedek, now a fine art teacher at the local elementary school, still living at number 26, right across the road from the Knavses' apartment. The British tabloid the *Daily Mail*, which recently published an article about Melania Trump, published the wrong information that the picture was of Melanija and her sister, Ines, when in fact she was with her friend Diana Kosar, today known as Diana Dernač.

Amalija Knavs and Olga Bedek, the mothers largely responsible for the girls landing their child modeling jobs, spent a lot of time together talking about their kids and husbands and their families spent evenings and weekends together. The two sewed all their children's clothes themselves, and used Ines, Melanija, and Nena whenever Jutranjka, which mostly produced children's clothes, needed child models. The mothers created the patterns for their children's appearances and accompanied them to the shows. The girls were never compensated for their work, but went purely for the fun of it and out of curiosity. In addition to Ljubljana they also appeared at fashion shows in Radenci, still today best known for its thermal baths, and even in Belgrade, the capital of Yugoslavia. Taking the train to Belgrade was in itself an experience and a reward for the girls.

Diana Dernač, who also appeared with Melanija as a child model, remembers that Melanija, who was soon to become enamored of the idea of becoming a model, was already very much at ease on the catwalk in those days. When other girls had stage fright and dreaded stepping out onto the catwalk, Melanija would be positively gleaming. At one of the shows Diana remembers searching in vain for her parents, who were cheering her on from the crowd, and forgetting to walk off the catwalk as rehearsed, but Melanija gently took her by the hand and walked the crying girl off the stage.

Melanija attended elementary school in her hometown. The school was named after the patriotic Sevnica resident Savo Kladnik, born July 1922, who was the leader of the opposition movement in Sevnica during the Second World War. A local informant tipped off the Gestapo about his whereabouts, and they locked him up in September 1942. The German occupiers then had him shot in Slovenia's second biggest city, Maribor, at the beginning of October of the same year, along with 143 other Slovenian prisoners. This sacrifice warranted Sevnica naming the elementary school that they opened in 1964 after him. In October 1969 they also unveiled a bronze bust of Savo, the work of sculptor Vladimir Štoviček, and a street was named after him in the new part of Sevnica.

Naselje Heroja Maroka, where Viktor and Amalija Knavs' family lived until 1995, is just a stone's throw from the Savo Kladnik Elementary School, a leisurely five-minute walk. At elementary school, sisters Ines and Melanija were taught the following subjects: Slovenian, Physics, Chemistry, Biology, Math, Geography, History, English, Physical Education, Art, Music, Technical Education, and Home Economics. The teachers also assessed behavior throughout.

Ines started school at the age of six in September 1974 and was a B student her first three years, before finishing the last five years of elementary school with As. She graduated from elementary school on 16 June 1982 with As in Slovenian, Chemistry, Biology, History, Art, Music, and Home Economics. The assessment of her behavior did not, however get top marks, but the teachers nonetheless remarked that she was "well prepared" for continuing her studies at the Secondary School for Design and Photography in Ljubljana.

Ines was a quiet and introvert student. She was extremely attached to her younger sister, and the same can be said of Melanija. The sisters were inseparable and after 1977 they attended the same school for a while. Incidentally that was the year of her future husband Donald's first marriage to Ivana Trump, and also the year Donald Jr. was born.

At school Melanija never wanted to be the center of attention, though her natural good looks and her elegant and unique style of dressing made her stand out immediately. School records indicate that she was of tranquil nature. She was a bright, hard-working, disciplined, practical, and gentle girl, who soon began sewing her own creations under the mentorship of her mother. Sketching various patterns and models of clothes was one of her favorite hobbies, and her mother gave her fabric and publications from fashion shows and trade fairs. It is therefore unsurprising that she had distinctively different clothes to other pupils. She had her own fashion sense, always adding something unusual to her clothes and wearing it with grace. Any bought clothes she always altered somehow, sewing something on them, hemming them, knitting woolen caps as accessories, and much more. She also knew exactly how to wear pegged jeans, jeans with a white stripe and knitted belt, and dresses with elastic waistbands – in short, whatever was in fashion. Despite the fact that she stood out, she never acted in a conceited way, though her English teacher of the time, Romana Ivačič, said she was *"always extravagant"* and *"even in elementary school dressed quite differently to all her peers."* Romana confesses that, at the time, this annoyed her, but that today she is proud to have taught English to the most famous Sevnica local in history.

Melanija was sociable, friendly with everyone, not just a select few, and acted as an intermediary, encouraging and helping her peers. She came across as perseverant, and always followed through on her promises. As she was very popular among her classmates, her teachers noted already in first grade that she had great leadership potential.

Her favorite subjects were Geography and Art, and she also loved to read, a fact noticed by her photographer Stane Jerko, who said she reminded him of a bookworm. The general consensus among her teachers was that Melanija Knavs expressed herself well, and she also kept a journal of her writing.

The most infamous former classmate of Melania Trump was probably Darko Slemenšek. He has been convicted of theft and robbery over forty times already. Their former-classmates say they no longer invite either of them to their reunions or other social gatherings.

Melanija confessed to her girlfriends on a number of occasions that she would like to move to Ljubljana. Mirjana Jelančič confirms how excited Melanija was about leaving for Ljubljana. As she completed her elementary education, she could hardly wait to move to the capital and try to establish herself as a designer and a model. She even attended art classes after school to prepare herself for such a career. Melanija and Mirjana Jelančič were very close at the time, and together they kept a scrapbook and a diary, a popular trend among Slovenian kids at the time.

When Melanija Knavs was at elementary school she was tiny, skinny, with gleaming blue eyes, beautifully maintained brown hair typically in bangs, though toward the end of school she began cutting her hair in layers to follow the trends of the era. She had a ballet bar in her room that she used for posture exercises and in general she took very good care of herself.

Melanija, however, was not really recognized in those days as an exceptional beauty. In her parents' eyes that title belonged to Ines, who had a great figure and was not as thin as Melanija. Ines was slightly unusual, but extremely attractive with long, brown hair, dark brown eyes, and remarkably "Asiatic" eyes. Ines also had a darker complexion than Melanija, and always used black eyeliner around her eyes.

Over the years, especially whilst studying in Ljubljana, her friends and locals from Sevnica attest that Ines Knavs became more and more withdrawn. Even at home, she would shut herself in her room, and some in Sevnica say she had certain psychological problems even at the age of ten. Her skin turned pale and she refused to talk with her friends from Sevnica. She now permanently lives in New York. When Melania's former friend Mirjana Jelančič saw a picture of Ines Knavs taken in New York, she could not believe it was her. A female relative who wishes to remain anonymous, says that there were rumors in the family that Ines was schizophrenic, something that some of her posts on social media posts also point to, as she has occasionally contradicted and attacked her very own words on her

Facebook profile and uploaded some rather unusual photographs. According to this same relative, Ines moved out
of the Trump Tower apartment into another Trump-owned
building in Manhattan about two years ago.

Both sisters took after their mother Amalija's beautiful
looks. Amalija was – in addition to being one of the nicest
mothers in the neighborhood – one of the prettiest women
in Sevnica. She looked after herself. She always walked to
work across the Sava River, meaning she started her day
with beneficial exercise. Amalija Knavs religiously wore
high heels, dressing herself and both her daughters mostly
in clothes she had made. While most other residents of the
neighborhood residents were asleep, a light could often be
seen in the Knavses' apartment, a sure sign that Amalija was
sewing.

Their apartment was rather colorful, with white furniture adoring a blue living room and a red kitchen, and
everything looked neat and tidy. The family had a color TV,
which was a true rarity in communist Slovenia, and was
considered a luxury item.

At school, Melanija was not as good a student as her
older sister Ines. Her best grades were in Geography and
Art, and these were also her favorite subjects. She began
learning English, which American journalists like to point
out she still hasn't entirely mastered today, in 5th grade. After finishing elementary school and receiving her final B-
average report card in June 1985, she followed her sister's
footsteps in taking the entrance exam to the Secondary
School for Design and Photography in Ljubljana. Ines had

got her enthusiastic about the school itself, but the course Melanija chose focused on industrial design, starting in the fall of 1985.

When Melanija and Ines were still young, before they started school and during their elementary years, Viktor Knavs often drove the family to visit his parents, who lived at Pod Pečico number 2 in nearby Radeče. There they would also meet up with Viktor's brother Herman and his family. At the family's old home in the southwest part of Radeče there was always good food, good cheer, music, songs, dancing, and great times. Grandpa Jožef played the accordion while Viktor sang. Herman's daughter Karmen was the same age as her cousin Ines, with whom she got into all sorts of trouble. They became Melanija's role models, explaining to her all the secrets of childhood. They romped and played in the nearby fields, sandboxes, trees, the forests, but the three girls rarely invited Herman's second child Sandi, six years Melanija's junior, to join their games.

The Knavses from Sevnica and Radeče were an example of concord between young and old. Only in the years around the Munich Olympics, so about 1972, did the Knavs family see less of each other, as Herman went to work in West Germany as 'Gastarbeiter', a temporary migrant worker. He worked there for a while at the well-known BMW factory, and later for a company that assembled furniture, outfitting the most elite rooms built for the Olympics. Even today Herman remembers every detail of the finishing work they did on the Russian and American Olympic rooms.

After returning to Radeče in 1974 he was able to build a house on Starograjska Street number 20 in the center of Radeče, and Viktor continued visiting his brother in the new house as well. While the brothers still got along, that is until the beginning of their arguments and lawsuits after the death of their father in 1989, the two families often also spent their summer vacations together. The Jutranjka factory had union-owned vacation apartments on the Croatian Riviera along the Adriatic Sea, in the resort of Červar near Poreč and the families of the brothers Knavs spent many a summer vacation there.

When Herman returned from Germany, the Knavs brothers put into action their most ambitious joint project just above banks of the Sava River in the heart of Radeče. They bought a boat shell from the renowned Ljubljana-based manufacturer Kliček, and set about fashioning a 4-seated powerboat. Herman is still proud of their accomplishment, as he told journalist Marjan Jerman of the now defunct Slovenian weekly *Več* in 2005, *"As soon as it floated on water we took it to the seaside. With a Yamaha engine it moved pretty fast."*

Were Melania Trump ever to return to Sevnica, which seems quite unlikely given what she said to her ex-boyfriend Jure Zorčič years ago in New York, she would no longer be staying in the neighborhood Naselje Heroja Maroka, where, upon new housing legislation introduced by the Minister of Environment and Spacial Planning Miha Jazbinšek after the country's independence in 1991, the Knavs family were able to buy off their apartment from the Jutranjka factory at a very low price. They then sold it for a nice profit, allowing them to complete their house in the Beverly Hills of Sevnica, the neighborhood of Ribniki.

The idea of building a house in this neighborhood came when their old neighbors and friends, Ana and Jože Dernač, built their own house and moved to Ribniki. They liked the new neighborhood, just under a mile away from where they lived until then, so they bought a piece of property and started building their house that they finished in 1995. It is a two-storey house, almost 30 feet high, with 4 rooms, a basement, and an attic. A large and beautiful balcony adorns the front facade. Most houses in the area were built between 1970 and 1980. There are also many much older buildings among them, but the Knavses' house really stood out as modern in comparison to others in the neighborhood. The Slovenian tradition has always been to build large, with as many rooms as possible, to ensure that several generations would be able to use the house. The Knavses house is of modest size by comparison, as if they had a hunch that they would one day be moving away. They chose with taste and distinction, and the house also differs from the neighboring ones because of the giant sticker outside warning would-be intruders that the house is protected by G7 and is under video surveillance. The camera is readily visible, as it is placed quite unattractively at the top of the balcony's wooden beam. There used to be several trees planted outside, but they have all been cut down now. There is not even a fence, so anyone snooping around the house would be immediately spotted from afar. Official evaluations place the value of the house at a little less than $80,000, though the same type of house in Ljubljana would be valued at much, much more.

When in town, Viktor Knavs enjoys spending time with his old friends from the Sava Car Club, since they all have in common a love for automobiles and speedway races, held every year in the nearby town of Krško. Viktor even advertised his company Knaus Haus at the race track in 1996, and was considered quite the connoisseur of antique cars. Even today there is an antique Mercedes parked in the driveway at Ribniki 21, covered with a white canvas tarp.

Standing out among the friends Viktor Knavs spent time with is Rihard Černigoj, three years his junior, a retired electrical engineer. He had apparently also worked as a personal driver like Viktor. Černigoj was born on 8 July 1944 in Ljubljana, and is now the head of the Slovenian Third Age University in Sevnica. Rihard also built his house in Ribniki, at number 18, the only wooden-framed house in the whole neighborhood. He refuses to give any statement to the media about the Knavs family, though he surely has a lot to say, including details about what he and his friend Viktor did as members of the Sevnica cell of the Slovenian Communist Party.

In preparing to write this book, the authors wanted to photograph the Knavs home at Ribniki 21, which is joint-owned by Viktor and Amalija Knavs. As the house has been shown a number of times in both Slovenian and foreign media, we were under the impression that such a picture would not prove controversial. Viktor, however, was in Slovenia at the time, and happened to be sitting on a bench outside the house when we took the picture, causing a bizarre and even dangerous turn of events. After snapping a picture of Viktor and his house, he jumped into his metallic brown Mercedes and took off after us like a bat out of hell. We did not notice him until he passed us on the open road toward nearby Krško and slammed on his brakes in front of us. It is only due to the quick thinking of our driver that we avoided hitting his car, or worse flying off the road or into oncoming traffic.

After this bizarre and negligent behavior, the situation got even worse as Viktor tried to get out of his car. From his livid, crazed gaze and flushed face it was clear that the the he was meaning to tackle the issue on a physical level. His size however, one might say he is actually fat, prevented him from climbing out of the car quickly enough, and we drove around him to avoid an altercation, and just kept driving ahead. We only managed to catch sight of Viktor hastily and with a bit of difficulty trying to get himself back into his Mercedes and take off after us again. After a few minutes later it seemed he came to his senses and gave up what could only be called a cinematic car chase. Nonetheless, it will be hard to forget this weird, unnecessary, uncalled for, and even extremely dangerous behavior on the part of Trump's father-in-law.

The Secondary School for Design and Photography in Ljubljana where Melanija enrolled in September 1985, has a long tradition reaching all the way back to 1766, when it was the first trade school to open in Ljubljana, then under control of the Jesuits, an extremely devout Roman Catholic order. The actual design syllabus of the school has its beginnings in the first year after the Second World War, when on 14 March 1946 the communist regime reformed the Jesuit school into an artistic trade school, whose main task was to prepare and equip its apprentices for independent design work, generate artistic leaders in trade and industry within the communist movement, and to generally raise the level of Slovenian craftsmanship.

The trade school had six divisions: Decorative Painting, Sculpture and Woodcarving, Interior Design, Pottery, Metalworking, and Women's Crafts. The curriculum focused primarily on the progress of crafts and trades, and less on developing industrial design, which was a consequence of the communist thinking about the primacy of an object's utility over its aesthetics. Nonetheless, the actual needs of Slovenian industry, especially exports, lead to the trade school's reform into a school of design, which in 1960 was reduced to three divisions instead of six: graphic design, textile design, and industrial design. Pupils do not specialize in their first year at the school and in addition to general courses there is a huge emphasis on artistic theory as a foundation for everything to come in the upper years. Regardless of the focus though, the curriculum in the upper years is split between theory and hands-on work at workshops, studios, and labs.

The photography program was added in 1981, and the school once again changed its name, becoming the Secondary School for Design and Photography. The school program, enrollment into which depended on the potential pupil's performance at a mandatory entrance exam, lasts for four years, and now includes the following four career tracks: Graphic Design, Industrial Design, Fashion Design, and Photography. It is located at Križanke, in the heart of the capital's historic center, in a former monastery with a stunningly designed courtyard, event hall, restaurant, church, and part of the original Ancient Roman town walls as it stands at the boundary between the medieval town of Ljubljana and the Roman town of Emona. Due to its rather unsuitable facilities within the former monastery, the school board has long sought a more appropriate location. Križanke is one of Slovenia's most beautiful cultural, historical, and architectural masterpieces but after the Second World War the communist regime forced the removal of the monks and expropriated the building for several secular institutions, the school among them.

Ines Knavs, who arrived in Ljubljana a few years before Melanija, enrolled in the school's industrial design program and later, unsuccessfully, continued at Ljubljana's Academy of Fine Arts. Melanija and her friend Nena Bedek were also interested in industrial design, and Melanija indeed enrolled in the program, while Nena decided instead on fashion design. As they prepared for the entrance exam, Melanija and Nena were at their wit's end all year. The exam, which included sections on Slovenian language and a practical test of artistic abilities, specifically in drawing, was quite demanding. It was held at the end of June 1985, right after graduation from elementary school, so the girls needed to prepare before they even finished classes for the year. After successfully passing, Melanija and Nena were both accepted into their respective programs, which, despite being different tracks, nonetheless included many of the same teachers.

It seems rather odd that Melanija Knavs opted for industrial design and not fashion, as she was rather obsessed with fashion and modeling, but it is likely that she considered industrial design as more attractive and more conducive to a wider array of artistic expression and career options. At the very least it promised a better chance of escaping Sevnica, via Ljubljana, and going into the world. Melania's present activities also seem to confirming that design is her field. As wife to billionaire Trump she can do pretty much whatever she wants, which, besides reading fashion magazine, seems to be designing her own line of jewelry, namely the brand Melania Timepieces & Fashion Jewelry, to which she added a line of skin care products containing caviar two years ago, the Melania Caviar Complexe C6 trade mark. Apparently she uses this caviar every evening to rub her son Barron William's skin, mini Donald, as she calls him, who otherwise *"bosses everyone around and keeps firing his nannies"*.

Lessons at the School for Design and Photography started at 7:10 every day and finished at 2:05 in the afternoon on some days and 2:55 on other days, as pupils were on a rotating schedule. Classes were usually 45 minutes long, with 5 minutes intervals between them, but studio, workshop, and lab classes lasted for a full hour. All the career tracks had a number of common general credits, namely Slovenian Language and Literature, English, Math and Descriptive Geometry, History and Art History, and Pre-military Education. Specialized courses included Fundamentals of Planar

Design, Plastic Design, Drawing and Calligraphy Technique, Interior Design, History and Development of Furniture, History of Design, Studio Drawing, and much else, and as usual, behavior was also graded in all four years. The school included carpentry, metalworking, ceramic, graphic, and photography workshops, as well as a modeling studio, but the physical education class was held at Tabor Hall in the center of Ljubljana, as there is no gym in Križanke.

It should be noted that it is impossible to obtain Melanija Knavs' grades from high school, as they have supposedly mysteriously disappeared from the school archives or the school's management prohibits access in a policy of personal data protection. Ines and Melanija must have been relatively good high-school students, proven by their successful completion of the extremely demanding university entrance exams at the Ljubljana Academy of Fine Arts and Architecture. It also helped that their father had rented and then bought them an apartment in the northern part of the capital, in a neighborhood of socialist-era apartment blocks. The building had five floors, and five stairwells, and the girls' address was Glinškova Ploščad 20. Though the apartment was modest, the fact that the Knavses had enough money to afford the extra rent in the capital proves that the family comfortably fitted into what was by socialist standards the upper middle class, as if having a house and a large antique Mercedes were not proof enough. Jure Zorčič, one of Melanija's first boyfriends, still remembers the apartment to this day and Peter Butoln, Melania's first boyfriend, likes to talk about the white sofa in the living room, where the potential First Lady of United States lost her virginity.

Working in Ljubljana as a traveling sales agent for the car sales company Slovenija Avto, Viktor spent a lot of time with his daughters, while their mother Amalija continued to work at the Jutranjka factory in Sevnica, joining them at weekends, where she spoiled her daughters with delicious cooking and did their laundry and ironing. It was rare for Viktor to return to Sevnica with the girls, as all signs point to the fact that they rather avoided their hometown. Thirty years later Melanija also spoke to the well-known American magazine *Harper's Bazaar* about her family's summer vacations on Croatia's Adriatic coast together with the family of the politician Matjaž Han, and about their skiing trips to Austria and Italy in winter.

During her time in high school, Melanija explored Ljubljana with her sister and friends, especially its historic part, which stretches along the banks of the river below Castle Hill, frequenting bars and cafés popular with Ljubljana's residents, such as Roža, Romeo, and Zlata Ladjica, and strolling along the famous bridges that crisscross the Ljubljanica River. Plečnikov Hram, the bar and restaurant located within Križanke, was a place that students of the design school avoided like the plague until their senior year, fearing the random chance encounter with one of their teachers, who claimed the place as their own; many a well-known bohemian from Ljubljana wet their lips sitting at its bar. Her friends and acquaintances do not recall Melanija Knavs having any episodes of errant behavior, nor do they remember her abusing drugs or alcohol at any time.

In high school Melanija meticulously looked after her looks and image, of course with her father's financial and organizational support. The leatherworking wizard Silva Njegač from Bukovci near Ptuj, an ancient Slovenian town located about an hour from both Ljubljana and Sevnica, talked about Melania to the local newspaper *Štajerski Tednik* in February of 2005, a month after her January wedding to Donald Trump. Silva sewed Melania's first leather clothing item back in 1987, when Melania was only seventeen. She remembers exactly the large black Mercedes out of which stepped the tall, dark-haired, makeup-free Melanija Knavs, radiating a natural beauty and turning heads at first glance. Viktor had of course driven his daughter to Ptuj in his Mercedes. Melanija told Silva that she was a big fan of leather clothes, and that she had heard about her workshop from her friends, then asking if she would sew something for her.

"It is always a pleasure to sew something beautiful for attractive girls like you," Silva answered, starting a collaboration that lasted for years, even after the model Melanija had already flown off to Milan, Paris, and New York. Silva Njegač says that Melanija would sketch the designs she wanted Silva to make, and that it was obvious that the girl attended design school.

Melanija stopped in to see Silva at least twice a year, even when she was already working abroad, usually during the summer and around Christmastime, often directly after touching down at the airport in Brnik – Silva always made time for her client immediately. Melanija's favorite color combinations were black, white, and beige and she most often ordered knee-length coats, skirts, pants, jackets, and purses. In 2002 Silva and Melania started discussing the possibility of a partnership where Silva would make her leather clothes, and Melania would market them under her own brand.

Silva Njegač's creations traveled to America twice; the first package got lost and was traced only after a second lot had already been made. After this, everything came to a halt. Silva does not know why, but Melania never called in again. Silva is, however, still in touch with Melania's parents.

Silva's notebooks also include Melania's measurements, and these are quite different to those published by the leading Slovenian women's magazine *Jana* in February 2005. Today Silva says that she regrets that the only records she has of Melania are her measurements; interestingly they never took a picture together.

In 1987, when Melanija Knavs was a in her third year at high school, she is said to have met Peter Butoln, who later went on to become a journalist and public relations adviser to prime minister Janez Drnovšek and his successor Anton Rop, now a businessman and entrepreneur. He is also supposedly the first man to have been intimate with Melanija. At least that is what he claimed to a journalist from a tabloid magazine *Suzy*, some 29 years later, in 2016.

Peter Butoln, who was Jure Zorčič's classmate in Poljane High School and drove a blue Vespa scooter, and Melanija Knavs met in a famous café called Konjski rep, located in the very center of Ljubljana where the iconic three bridges called Tromostovje cross the river Ljubljanica. It was springtime and after just two weeks they began dating. Butoln told the Slovenian media that their first romantic encounter happened at her apartment in Glinškova Ploščad. Today he says she was smart and intelligent, not at all ditzy. She did speak however, of wanting to leave Slovenia and go abroad, because nothing ever happened in Slovenia. According to Butoln, he never perceived her as someone who above all wanted money, a 'gold-digger', but it could be something that was rooted deep inside her, since she always had money and even paid for drinks on occasion.

Their relationship did not last very long; they supposedly broke up that autumn when Butoln left for his mandatory military service. When he returned a year later, in 1988, and even during his service, he called her by phone but she never answered. On one occasion, however, her sister Ines picked up the phone. According to Butoln, this led to his relationship with Ines, who at the time was already studying architecture. Butoln says, he and Ines were never a couple, but he claims that they too were intimate, in that same apartment that the Knavs family rented in Ljubljana. So Peter Butoln was the man who slept with both sisters, the future Melania Trump and Ines Knavs. He also likes to say within his inner circle that Ines was a lot more passionate in bed than Melanija, who simply "laid there." Apart from that, the two years older Ines also had larger breasts.

And while Melanija and Peter Butoln never saw or spoke to each other again, he and Ines Knavs, by then already Ines Knauss, spoke on the phone for the last time in 2012. What happened was the following, after Anton Rop's government coalition with the LDS (Liberal Democracy of Slovenia Party) fell apart in 2004 and the conservative right-wing opposition led by Janez Janša took office, Peter Butoln, as a former consultant to Rop, was jobless. Because Melanija was already Donald Trump's partner at that point, Butoln tried to contact her, so she might help him continue his career as a public relations consultant in the United States. He called Viktor Knavs by phone. Viktor remembered him as Melanija's former boyfriend who used to visit her on Glinškova Ploščad but did not want to give him Melania's phone number, instead giving him the Slovenian mobile phone number of Ines. Peter Butoln called her and, as mentioned, they remained in contact until four years ago.

Among other things, Ines confided in Peter that Melanija has cut all ties with Slovenia and only speaks English with her Slovenian friends. She also told him that Donald and Melania only see each other a few times a month; the rest of the time Trump is too busy rushing around about his business. Butoln also likes to brag about how Ines also told him things that could potentially destroy the Trumps' marriage if they ever became public. Ines also talked about her own life in the United States and has even mentioned working for Vogue and taking on the occasional interior design jobs for some of Donald Trump's clients and business associates.

Peter Butoln worked as an independent entrepreneur until 2010, when he shut down his business because of a divorce from his second wife and a bitter custody battle over his two children. He claims that everything he has said about Melania is the absolute truth and he is prepared to take a lie detector to prove it. It was precisely because of the legal battle with his ex-wife that Butoln decided to share his story about Melania Trump with *Suzy* magazine. He was told to approach them by the famous Slovenian media and political marketing consultant Sebastjan Jeretič, who advised him to strike a deal with the executive editor of *Suzy* magazine, Barbra Jermann. He would share his story with the magazine and in turn they would help him media wise with his legal troubles connected with his former wife. Butoln says he kept his end of the bargain but the magazine did not. Once he had told his story about Melanija, his own story no longer interested them.

Peter Butoln has not heard from Ines since 2012 when, without warning, her Slovenian phone number became unreachable. He still keeps the number and has shown it to the author. He also showed this same number to the *New York Times* reporters when they visited him in Ljubljana. They called Ines Knauss together then but there was no answer. After Butoln related his story to the media, Melania Trump said nothing, while Ines Knauss responded with a Facebook post, stating, *"Peter, don't lie!"* Butoln says Ines' reaction was to be expected as she had never told Melania, that she too had slept with him.

He also claims to have photographs of Melania in a swimsuit and topless, but refuses to show them, unless he is paid handsomely for them. Anonymously of course, because, as he says, he has fond memories of their time together. As proof of their relationship, he showed the media a postcard that Melania sent him from vacation to his address on Neubergerjeva Street in Ljubljana. He is planning on entering the blue Vespa Piaggio that he drove Melania around Ljubljana on into an online auction with an initial price of 10,000 euros. Perhaps Vladimir Putin would be interested in owning a Vespa from Melania Trump's first man, he could even give it as a gift it to Donald Trump later on, he adds humorously. Peter Butoln is currently in the process of trying to sell a mobile application for audio advertising for 2 million euros to the state owned Telekom Slovenija, a deal which is supposedly being lobbied for by the previously mentioned Veljko Karas.

When Melanija Knavs successfully graduated from high school, she first went on a school trip to Dubrovnik in Croatia and then enrolled on a university course in Architecture in the fall of 1989. In the meantime, she participated at a competition to become the face of Cinecittà films in Rome. It was not exactly a beauty pageant, more of a personality contest, and Melanija ended up winning. In a peculiar irony, Cinecittà, today Europe's largest film studio that the famous Italian director Federico Fellini called home, was founded by the Fascist dictator Benito Mussolini to make his propaganda films and after the Second World War served as a refugee camp for a while. So, while Melanija's mother Amalija was born in exile a mere two months after the fall of Hitler's Third Reich close to a refugee camp in Austria, her daughter won a beauty contest in Mussolini's old studio also turned into a post-bellum refugee camp.

Before Melanija could even begin studying architecture at Ljubljana University, she needed to pass the Academy's entrance exam like everyone else. This was much more than a mere formality, but a true test of grit. It was an evaluation of the candidate's talent for artistic understanding and expression, their spatial reasoning and their sense and awareness about current issues and theories in architecture. The test was made up of two parts, the first being a comprehensive written exam on spatial visualization, artistic expression, and spatial composition, while the second part included an interview with the candidate, whose personal characteristics, motives, interests, and awareness were tested. The exam lasted 3 days, with artistic tests in the morning and interviews in the afternoon. Melanija passed the exam.

The future Mrs. Trump entered the Faculty of Architecture and Civil and Geodetic Engineering at the University of Ljubljana, the oldest and largest higher educational institute in Slovenia, in the 1989. The architecture program, which despite the joint name was separate from the civil and geodetic engineering programs, included straight architecture (chosen by around 55% of students), urban studies (27%), and design (18%). Melanija chose the latter, but she failed already in the first year of study. In her freshman year, the 19-year old Melanija Knavs attended lectures on the following subjects: Elements of Architecture, Fine Arts, Fundamentals of Technical Mechanics, Architectural Construction, Descriptive Geometry, Mathematics, and an ideological (i.e. "Communist") elective credit called "General Partisan Resistance and Social Self-protection." Even having failed two exams, Melanija could have made it to her sophomore year, but would have needed to complete a successful one-month internship at a building site and handed in her journal about it.

The drop out rate at the School of Architecture was around 50%, and Melanija Knavs was among those the school had weeded out. Given that she had been a hard-working and good student in high school, and that modeling did not at the time take up that much of her time, we can only assume that she was not cut out for such a demanding course; she became – and remained – a college dropout.

Later, in America, after meeting Donald Trump and officially becoming his partner, Melania Knauss told the media that she had obtained her degree in architecture and design. This was almost certainly done in consultation with Trump and his advisors, as they were desperate to give off the impression that the Slovenian model was not just beautiful, but also smart and well-educated. Even as recently as June 2014 some Slovenian media outlets, for example the widely read online portal Siol.net, which is owned by Telekom Slovenija, reported without questioning that Melania Knauss *"became a much sought out model in Paris and Milan, after her graduation from Ljubljana University."*

But things got complicated when some Slovenian journalists found out and reported that Melania Knauss was lying to the American media about her education. Since her thesis could not be found in the university system or the country's national register of publications, journalists started asking for direct and official answers from the leadership of the Faculty of Architecture at the University of Ljubljana as to whether Melanija Knavs was their graduate or not. The Faculty stayed tight-lipped, citing Slovenia's strict legislation on personal data protection as a reason, maintaining that it was Melania Knauss' personal business. Her sister Ines' thesis could not be found either. After that Melania began saying that she had only studied architecture but chose to prioritize her modeling career instead. Some classmates' testimonials even say that she was considered the "queen of her class," until one day she just disappeared from lectures and discussions and never turned up again.

The late Vojteh Ravnikar, legendary Slovenian architect and professor at the Faculty of Architecture, reported fifteen years ago to Slovenian columnist Marko Crnkovič that Melanija Knavs had been his student. He did though always use the word "it seems" meaning that he was not certain. In his characteristic humor he remarked that it would be great if he could remember a good story about her so and show off with it, but sadly, he does not. He could not remember what she was like at all.

The very year that Melanija Knavs in Ljubljana "became and remained a college dropout," her future husband Donald Trump almost went bankrupt for the first time. Newspapers all over the world, including Slovenian *Delo*, *Dnevnik*, and *Večer*, all reported on the bankruptcy of one of the best known and wealthiest Americans, but no one knows if Melanija Knavs read about it at the time. Most likely not, since, as her friends and acquaintances say, she was only interested in her modeling career.

In June 1990 Donald Trump's entrepreneurial fate was in the hands of his creditors, and his case turned into one of the biggest dramas on Wall Street. Trump first made headlines due to his divorce from the notorious Ivana Trump, then the media scandal turned into a financial problem that was about to affect all of Wall Street. The largest banks in America, which had financed the Trump empire, hastily met to discuss whether to grant him another loan and thus help him climb out of his troubles, and then sell off several assets and companies to repay his debt, or whether they should pull the plug and force him into bankruptcy proceedings. Trump, who was also known as a reckless spender on a personal level, including among other things a million-dollar yacht, a personal jet and helicopters, and several eminently luxurious mansion and other pieces of real estate, at first denied any financial troubles, but then suddenly reported that he was selling his yacht and airline, but just to free up some cash. Financial analysts showed that the problem stemmed from the excessive debts he racked up building his latest hotel and casino in Atlantic City. The hotel and casino would have to generate a million dollars a day in order for him to cover the costs.

Trump eventually admitted that he was negotiating with banks on how to solve the problem. The value of his hotels' bonds fell sharply, and his investors began to seriously worry about their money. Several cynical journalists kindly and publicly advised Trump's outgoing wife Ivana, who had launched a divorce suit, to take Donald's offer of $25 million and not demand a single cent more, as she would have a hard time collecting even that much; financial experts were reporting at the time that Trump owed the banks a total of 3 billion dollars.

Chapter 4

THE SOCIALIST BELLE AND SMUGGLED JEANS

Stane Jerko, already popular among the biggest stars of Slovenian show business, and today, as so generously claimed by the tabloids, a living legend in the photography world, was leaving the Festival Hall in Ljubljana after a fashion show. A slim young woman with long hair was calmly but curiously leaning against the gate outside the hall and, though she was modestly dressed, she immediately grabbed his attention. She was attractive and had all the appropriate measurements; in fact she was exactly the type that Jerko, already with the budding eye of a professional photographer, had been looking for. And he most often found what he was after. Without hesitation, he walked right up to her, introducing himself and suggested they try making a few test shots.

It was a freezing cold night in January 1987, and the young woman was Melanija Knavs. She was not yet seventeen at the time, a sophomore at Ljubljana's Secondary School for Design. Melanija trusted him, probably because

Jerko was holding a camera and had come out of the hall where a fashion show had just ended.

Four weeks later she paid Jerko a visit at his studio in northern Ljubljana where he still works today and 20 years later, a week after Melania and Donald Trump's wedding, Jerko reminisced that back then Melanija was still *"quite timid,"* which of course, as he knows well, *"was nothing out of the ordinary."*

She had done her own hair and makeup, and had brought her own clothes to the shoot. *"She was extremely quiet, thin, and didn't appear to have any lofty modeling ambitions. Melanija seemed more of a bookworm to me,"* said Stane Jerko.

Before getting started, Jerko carefully wrote down Melanija Knavs' measurements, on what can today be considered an almost legendary piece of paper. Height 176.5 cm (5 feet 9.5 inches), weight 55 kg (121 lbs), chest 85 centimeters (31.5 inches), waist 65 centimeters (25.5 inches), hips 93 centimeters (36.5 inches), age 17, and a few other photographic details, adding for posterity, *"Spring 87, test shots for model"*.

Later Jerko told the media that Melanija, *"lived in Ljubljana with her sister, Ines, and they were quite attached to one another."* Every weekend, though, Jerko says, *"they went back home to their native Sevnica,"* which wasn't entirely true. Melanija and Ines actually lived in Ljubljana together with their father Viktor, and the girls' mother Amalija Knavs would come to Ljubljana every weekend to cook, clean, and iron. Only rarely did the trio of Melanija, Ines, and Viktor set off over the weekend for Sevnica, as, according to Viktor's younger brother Herman, they were *"happy to be away from their hometown."*

Why the ever polite Stane Jerko told this to the media is unknown, but it is probably the case that he did not exactly invent it, but that this was the side of the story he was told, "fed" by Melanija during their photo sessions, making her come across as wholesome and pleasant as possible in front of the famous and influential photographer.

Melanija's second photo shoot at Stane Jerko's studio was to take pictures for the fashion magazine *Maneken*. The shots, according to Jerko were *"even better"* than the first time, as Melanija *"was relaxed and worked more confidently in front of the camera."*

Stane Jerko was also known for meticulously touching up the pictures he took, since *"all women like to be pretty,"* a fact he once disclosed to the Slovenian tabloid Lady. In those times this was achieved by adjusting the light, the exposures, and the development of the film, today it is of course done digitally. *"If you have even a little knack, if you know your colors, the human anatomy, and technology, you can do whatever you want,"* Jerko once said. How, where, and how much he had to touch up Melanija Knavs' pictures remains a mystery, but Stane Jerko showed her first photos to a few fashion agencies. They were *"interested,"* he later confided, but he never saw Melanija Knavs in his studio in Ljubljana again. He did later notice her, as he admitted, in *"some advertisements and then in* [the magazine] *Jana's Look of the Year competition, where she and Mojca Mladenovič shared second place."* This took place in June 1992, in the Slovenian coastal town of Portorož, and the Look of the Year competition still stands out as one of the key breakthroughs in Melanija Knavs' modeling career.

Due to that fateful meeting that night outside the Festival Hall in Ljubljana, Stane Jerko claims the prestigious title of having 'discovered' the future Melania Trump, who, for her part, has also admitted as much to the Slovenian press. This she confirmed years ago when speaking to Jožica Brodarič on the cult Slovenian fashion show *Trend*, saying that the first to notice *"her pretty face and model's figure amid the crowd of young girls"* was the photographer Stane Jerko.

Stane Jerko returned her the compliment a month or so after her marriage with Trump in Florida, speaking in a short interview for Slovenia's most popular weekly magazine for women, *Jana*. He said specifically that, *"in America Melania has turned from that scared but pretty little girl into a very mature and confident woman, who knows exactly what she wants."*

Twenty eight years later Stane Jerko sold some of the pictures he took of Melanija during those first two sessions in his Ljubljana studio to the British *Daily Mail*, which was doing a report on Melania. Rumor had it that he received, at least by Slovenian standards, quite a sum of money for these pictures. But these rumors of extravagant earnings seem shaky at best. At the end of January 2016 Stane Jerko was heard complaining that the tabloid, to which he sent 40 pictures, had still not paid him and that if and when they would, the sum would not even be enough for a nice trip somewhere for him and his wife.

When the *Daily Mail* published these pictures, well-known Slovenian columnist Marko Crnkovič cynically wrote on his blog Fokuspokus.si that, *"if you ask me, these pictures look ridiculous. A socialist beauty in high-end Yugoslav threads that wouldn't have turned my head even back then. Dressed as if for aerobics, with smuggled jeans* (Marko Crnkovič paused here to remember the throngs of Slovenians who, during the times of Yugoslavia's closed borders, smuggling denim jeans from nearby Italy, most notably from the city of Trieste), *and espadrilles!"*

Melanija Knavs and Jožica Brodarič first met on the weekly infotainment show *Studio City*, where Brodarič was filming a spot on studio fashion. Once a month she wrote the screenplay for a three-minute spot that was then directed by famous Slovenian movie and TV directors and slotted into *Studio City*.

The scenario this time was dedicated to professional women who also care about fashion, and were dressed in clothes for professionals from Mura, the then most famous Slovenian textile producer and also one of the most established brands in former Yugoslavia. The common thread of the fashion ad was a President who was a woman and the President would wear Mura clothes. To get a model, Brodarič turned, as always, to one of Ljubljana's fashion agencies, this time contacting the agent Marina Masowietsky, owner of the agency MCM, who operated from her old high-ceilinged town apartment on Pražakova Street in downtown Ljubljana.

"Hi, Marina. Hey, I need another model. You have anyone new for me? Someone who hasn't been on TV yet. She'll be wearing Mura, and, you know, she'll have to work for free, as our

famous television station doesn't pay a dime. It'll be a great way for her to get some exposure."

"OK, Jožica, no problem. I'll send you this new one we have from Sevnica. But at least send her home with an outfit, will you?"

"Sure," Jožica assured Marina Masowietsky, who would later play a much more visible role in Melanija Knavs' fashion career. One women's outfit from Mura those days cost roughly half a month's paycheck for an average worker at Jutranjka, where Melanija's mother Amalija was working.

So she sent the unknown model Melanija Knavs. Andrej Košak, the director who later directed *Outsider*, one of the most celebrated Slovenian movies of all time, was the one to direct the spot.

By the way, later, when *Outsider* became a real hit, it was revealed that Košak never actually finished directing the movie, with the role of director taken on by the main actor Davor Janjić, otherwise from Sarajevo, then living with the TV producer Urška Žnidaršič, who was responsible for the show *Trend*. Košak apparently had some problems with alcohol and perhaps even drugs at the time.

Brodarič and Košak came up with a scenario where the model played the President, so they rented a plane at the nearby Brnik Airport, a fancy limousine, and a huge office in a building protected as a national monument, namely the National and University Library of Ljubljana. National television had plenty of funds back in those days, and the show's budget was never an issue. The model Melanija Knavs, decked out in a Mura business suit, stepped out of the plane onto a red carpet as the President, then took a seat in the limo, waving in a dignified manner to a supposed crowd the whole time. Upon reaching the antiquely decorated office at the National Library, Melanija as the President took a solemn presidential oath. To make the spot as interesting as possible, and to lend it an air of authenticity, Andrej Košak did some digging in the archives at TV Slovenija and edited into the spot some clips of Americans waving to their president, so the whole thing came off looking to Studio City viewers as if Melanija Knavs was playing the role of President of the United States in the ad.

The Slovenian magazine *Stop* also published a few stills from the spot of Melanija Knavs in Mura's professional suits.

Looking back, it is of course, an amazing coincidence that, back then, as a completely unheard of model doing a short spot for Slovenian national television, she played the imaginary role of the US President and today, more than twenty years later, she is a serious contender for role of First Lady.

The show *Trend* is long gone, the Mura factory went bankrupt and was closed down, however, Studio City is still on air every Monday evening.

The now seventy-eight-year old Stane Jerko enjoys his reputation as a legendary Slovenian fashion photographer and still snaps the occasional picture, even though he has been officially retired for fifteen years. He is happy and satisfied that clients still turn to him, as cannot imagine a life without photography. He still remembers his golden age when *"even the models in Slovenia could live off of their work.*

Now they think of modeling as something to do while they study, and leave the industry as soon as they get a [real] *job."*

His first official model was his schoolmate and later for many years the prima donna of the Slovenian pop music scene, Marjana Deržaj. After her came a whole slew of Slovenian belles, including Anka Senčar and Bernarda Marovt, the only two Slovenian models who enjoyed real success abroad (Anka Senčar lives in Egypt and Bernarda Marovt in Milan), singers, starlets, and even several Slovenian men, including the current President of Slovenia, Borut Pahor, who was also a model years ago. Jerko's career breakthrough came with his photographs the renowned fashion designer from Ljubljana Alja Košak in her famous hats. Košak made hats for Jovanka Broz, the last wife of the Yugoslavian dictator Josip Broz Tito, and even for Queen Elizabeth II.

Stane Jerko, who otherwise does a good job of keeping up with the times, insisted on analog photography for a long time, saying as a professional that, *"early digital cameras were extremely unreliable It was not possible to create quality photos with them, and they were also expensive."*

Chapter 5

THE WORLD
OF GLITZ AND GLAM

"For a long time the world of high fashion, catwalks, and top models smiling at us from ads in luxury publications and appearing in the most influential TV commercials around the world was almost unattainable for Slovenian girls. The handful of beauty pageants that had been organized so far in Slovenia were not quite the same as high fashion and the world of elite models which operate in a completely differently way to the much more trivial and frivolous world of pageants." This was the introduction to a call for applications published on 11 March 1992 in the magazine Jana, which pompously and even somewhat patriotically declared on its front cover that *"Young Beauties are Marching into Europe!"* The editors at *Jana* had already added a banner right above the announcement in the title that read that this was *"an opportunity you must read!"*

The Republic of Slovenia, at that point not yet a full year into its independence, explaining the hint of patriotism, was *"marching with its girls to the summit of international modeling – This, the first Slovenian and international campaign to find top models – the magazines Jana and Interdesign will be choosing Slovenian candidates for Look of the Year, and girls who will carry the reputation of Slovenian charm to Paris, Milan, and Vienna."*

Interdesign was, at the time, the fashion agency of Marina Masowietsky, later an important manager in Melanija Knavs' career. Its official address was at Trnovski Pristan number 6 in Ljubljana. Apart from Interdesign, Maria Masowietsky owned two other agencies, MCM, or Model Casting and Management, which she claimed was the first Slovenian modeling agency with international connections, and Model Group, a scouting agency that placed its girls in *"events worldwide."* Model Group also based in Ljubljana, on Pražakova Street. Marina later gave that agency to the famous Slovenian model Maja Bulc.

Time, of course, tells its own story. Melanija Knavs, who did not even win the Look of the Year competition, has, some 23 years later, as Melania Trump brought the reputation of Slovenian charm to the threshold of the White House in Washington.

"The only competition so far," the editorial in Jana continued with an air of pedagogic historicity, *"to launch our (Slovenian) girls into the world of professional international modeling has been the Look of the Year competition. It was organized by the Zagreb-based women's periodical Svijet and was a competition to find the most promising faces (and figures) from throughout former Yugoslavia. It is true that several Slovenian girls sign up for this competition every year and some have achieved enviable success."*

In fact, the previous year's winner of Look of the Year was Ljubljana native Nataša Budnar, who readers of *Jana* had *"got to know very well."* This was something the editors at Jana were proud of.

"But there has never before been a true Slovenian competition – in Slovenia – for this prestigious title. Of course," Jana continues, *"quite a few Slovenian girls have gone on to enjoy admirable achievements, with Bernarda Marovt leading the pack. In conversations she* [Bernarda] *has often mentioned that Slovenian girls are almost perfect for international recognition in this prestigious field, but that sadly there is no proper opportunity for their charm to see the light of day in any organized way,"* the experts at Jana admitted.

Bernarda Marovt can truly pride herself with numerous admirable awards, mostly due to her modeling career. She still lives in Milan and only comes to Slovenia a few times per year, but those of us who are middle-aged remember her well as the former Miss Yugoslavia, remember her naked photos from the Yugoslavian cult magazine *Start*, and remember her from countless advertisements and successful walks down the catwalks of foreign fashion centers. Bernarda Marovt was Italy's top model in 1990 and top model in Europe in 1992, so, right at the time when Melanija Knavs was starting to make an impact on the Slovenian modeling scene. That same year Bernarda Marovt became the most photographed face in the world (a title that a few years later went Princess Diana), and in 2000 the magazine Jana declared no less than Slovenian beauty of the century.

Some younger Slovenian models who worked in Milan at the time when Bernarda Marovt was already a star complained that she would barely say hello to them in the hallways of Riccardo Gay's modeling agency, even though she knew very well that they were fellow Slovenians. To Bernarda Marovt they were dangerous younger competition in the highly competitive world of fashion.

"Slovenia is now its own country," the editors at Jana continued patriotically. *"Numerous reputable and famous European advertising agencies expressed a lot of interest in organizing and selecting the winners in the first real Slovenian Look of the Year competition, the winners who will be able to take their place alongside the most well-known and popular European models, sharing with them the market, the fame – and the money. The earnings of the best in this otherwise extremely difficult and demanding profession are of course astronomic, and most ordinary mortals get dizzy just thinking about the sums. The best-known models in Europe can currently make up to $20,000 a day! You read right, through, of course, only a handful will ever reach the top league for such earnings. So it is about time that charming, long-legged, and appropriately slim Slovenian girls start making their mark in Europe as top models!"*

The Slovenian judges of the Look of the Year contest were helped in their search for these charming, long-legged, and appropriately slim Slovenian girls who were supposed to march on Europe by three well-known, at that time one might even say most famous, European fashion agencies, namely the Parisian Metropolitan, Wiener Modellsekretariat from Vienna, and Milan-based R.V.R. Reclame Model Management.

Unarguably the most famous and also the most expensive face of the Parisian Metropolitan was the German supermodel Claudia Schiffer, who at the time could earn between 20 and 22 thousand German Marks a day. The agency also promised the winner of the Slovenian Look of the Year competition in Portorož a three-year contract with travel and living expenses paid in Paris, where they would *"intro-duce her to the world of their sparkling business,"* as they prided themselves. To make the prize seem even more attractive, not to mention credible, *Jana* ran a special page just for a copy of the future contract.

Claudia Schiffer was one of the supermodels making up the Big Six, along with Cindy Crawford, Naomi Camp-bell, Linda Evangelista, and Christy Turlington, and Kate Moss. These were the women beyond the lens and on the catwalks that the young Slovenian beauties envied, but even more, looked up to with respect, awe, and ambition. Though Claudia Schiffer was German, a European, it was Cindy Crawford who made the biggest impression on Slo-venians, with her 86-66-89 measurements and the owner of one of the most successful, wealthiest, and most recogniz-able faces and bodies in the fashion industry, capped off by the beauty mark above her lip; the stunner who adorned the covers of more magazines than any other model in the world.

Cynthia Ann Crawford was born in DeKalb Illinois on 20 February 1966 and is 4 years and 2 months older than Melanija. From her early childhood she was picked on be-cause of the mole above her lip, which was even edited out of her photos at the beginning of her career, even on her debut cover shot for *Vogue*.

Cindy Crawford began her modeling career at the age of sixteen, much later than Melanija Knavs started hers. She was spotted by a photographer from a local newspaper while Cindy was at a summer job husking corn. Her first shots had so much potential that, at the age of seventeen, she applied for the Look of the Year competition hosted by the influential fashion agency Elite and won runner up, just like Melanija Knavs did at the Look of the Year competition in Portorož. Following the competition Cindy Crawford came under the protection of Elite, and remained loyal to the agency for a number of years. The first foreign agency that signed Melanija Knavs was the Italian agency Riccardo Gay from Milan.

Despite her promising modeling career and ambitions, Cindy Crawford tried not to neglect her studies. In fact, she was the valedictorian at her graduation from DeKalb High School in 1984. This accomplishment earned her a scholarship to study Chemical Engineering at Northwestern University, where she stayed only one semester, before leaving school to move to New York and focus on modeling. This is yet another similarity to Melanija Knavs, who also did well in her Secondary School for Design, but soon gave up on her university studies.

Global fashion fame soon followed for Cindy Crawford. In the 1990s she appeared on the covers of fashion magazines and trend-setting publications with the largest readerships, such as *Vogue*, *W*, *People*, *Harper's Bazaar*, *Elle*, *Cosmopolitan*, *Allure*, and over a thousand others! It would be hard to find a catwalk at any relatively well-known fashion house that has not hosted the sexy brunette. Cindy Crawford's incredible career saw her debut clothes for Gianni Versace, Calvin Klein, Chanel, Ralph Lauren, Karl Lagerfeld, and Escade, and serve as spokeswoman for cosmetics companies

Revlon and Maybelline, as well as watchmakers Omega. She also worked for Pepsi.

At 5 feet 9 inches tall, 130 lbs, and a size 6 she was a whole new type of supermodel. At first she went by the nickname Baby Gia. In July 1988, a year after Ljubljana-based photographer Stane Jerko discovered and first photographed the shy Melanija Knavs, Crawford was a step ahead of her, as she became the first supermodel to pose fully nude for *Playboy*. Ten years later she once more posed for *Playboy*, this time in even more provocative positions.

Her workout videos became a commercial success, as did her Cindy Crawford's Basic Face program on makeup, but her movie career never really took off. Like so many famous beauties before her, Cindy Crawford could not resist the charm of TV and Hollywood. For many years she hosted *House of Style* on the then extremely popular TV channel MTV. Later she earned a leading role, of course as the femme fatale, in the 1995 film *Fair Game*, with the leading role played William Baldwin. The movie was a total flop, panned by critics and audiences alike. She tried again a few years later in *The Simian Line* (2000), which was also never a success, though critics were not as negative about her performance this time around. Cindy went on to play a few minor roles after that, but eventually completely gave up on acting.

Even though her acting career was a failure, the beauty of Cindy Crawford's face was impossible to overlook. *Playboy* put her on its list of the 100 sexiest stars of the 20th century, something Melanija Knavs missed out on by a long shot.

When Cindy Crawford took her last steps on the catwalk, she did not retire or marry rich, but continued with her business career. In 2005, the same year Melanija Knavs, by then Melania Knauss, married Donald Trump, Crawford worked with the Swiss pharmacist Jean-Louis Sebagh to establish her cosmetics line Meaningful Beauty. Although in adverts for Meaningful Beauty Crawford often assured that the melon extracts and other ingredients led to a more youthful appearance, Crawford admitted in public several times that she had also helped herself with plastic surgery, including botox, collagen, and vitamin injections, first going under the knife at the age of twenty-nine.

Crawford also brought out with her own line of furniture called the Cindy Crawford Home Collection, and shortly after married the Hollywood star Richard Gere. When their marriage fell apart, she remarried in 1998 to the former model and current restaurateur and owner of the Gerber Spirits brand, Rande Gerber. She has two children with Gerber. Presley Walker and Kaia Jordan, and they live in Malibu, California. Cindy Crawford once said that Malibu was her dream place to live, with the constant sound of relaxing waves.

The Parisian agency Metropolitan obviously did not want to leave anything to chance, to the whims of a neophyte, to any sort of embarrassments or lack of fashion and beauty know-how on the part of the Slovenian organizers, or even having to put up with hidden favorites or ulterior motives, promises, or debts, so it immediately announced its own member of the competition's jury.

The Viennese agency, with its somewhat bureaucratic-sounding name Wiener Modellsekretariat, represented at the time 250 of the most enviable top models from all over the world, and let the Slovenian organizers know that they prefer to discover their girls on their own, take a few test shots, and only then, if the girls prove themselves, arrange for the best possible jobs. It seems Vienna trusted Slovenians even less than Paris did.

The Viennese agency could boast that it was not merely a fashion agency, as the girls it represented often found big money in commercials and movie roles. The contract for cooperating in the beauty contest in Portorož was in Vienna signed of behalf of Wiener Modellsekretariat by Andrea Weilder who also became a member on the final jury. The Viennese had obviously placed their money on the runner-up, whom they would then announce themselves and invite to Vienna. There, as they said, the chosen girl would live in an apartment owned by the agency while they took her test shots. They also offered a special prize, namely two essential items for any up-and-coming model, composite shots and a book, photographic and textual content that all models need in order to land any kind of deal within the industry. Under normal circumstances, this would cost a girl between three and four thousand Deutschmarks apiece, a price certainly out of reach for any of the ordinary candidates for the Slovenian Look of the Year competition. Nonetheless, without these two essential items a career on the catwalks and in front of the cameras was simply impossible.

The offer from Milan-based R.V.P. Reclame Model Management was almost identical to that of the Wiener

Modellsekretariat, just that the Lombardians placed their bets on the third-placed girl, promising to fly her to and put her up in Milan, take her test shots, and put together composite shots and a book for her.

To apply years to the Look of the Year contest in Portorož, the girls had to be Slovenian citizens aged between 15 and 23. Any girls under the age of 18 had to have their parent's permission. At the time Melanija was 22.

In addition to the age restriction, height and size were also conditions, as candidates could not be shorter than 173 cm (5 foot, 8 inches). Organizers also made an appeal to *"spontaneity, confidence, and charm,"* while it wasn't necessary that the future models were also classically beautiful. Nonetheless, they needed *"to have that special something that radiates into the camera and that can attract experienced photographers, hair stylists, and makeup artists."* At the time full lips were especially sought after, and some agencies also insisted on light eyes.

We can get some idea about what Melanija Knavs (176 cm or 5 foot 9 inches tall) was like at the time from the words of the well-known Austrian and German fashion agent Wolfgang Schwarz, owner of the former agency The Girls & The Boys, who met Melanija Knavs in spring of 1993, less than a year after the competition in Portorož. At the time Schwarz was also a representative for the American agency Elite in Vienna.

"She had nothing, never put in any effort, never tried to give her best, was quiet and cold the whole time, and never radiated any energy."

In private circles Wolfgang Schwarz uses even mode sordid language, not only calling her a *"dead fish,"* but adding that she was *"very stupid"* and that it was *"extremely difficult to work with her." "Top model in Europe? I beg your pardon? No, never,"* Schwarz later commented.

In the twelve-second video that was shot back then by television director Aleksander Šmuc in Portorož, in front of the door of the hotel Emona in Bernardin, and in which Melanija does a brief walk in front of the camera and says a few words, one can get a real sense of her figure, ambition and desire to become a model. Šmuc says today that this is one of his private recordings, not owned by the Slovenian National Television (RTV Slovenija), where he is employed. He is hoping that some American network might be interested in buying the video recording for several tens of thousands of dollars.

Melanija Knavs, along with all the other candidates that applied to the contest in Portorož, had to fill out a special application form published in the magazine *Jana*. The organizers slightly patronizing instructions, as if addressing teenagers, explained that applicants should cut the application from the magazine, fill it out carefully, and send it off with their photographs that should not be more than six months old. They were required to send a face shots and a full-body portrait, if possible but not obligatory in a swimsuit. At the time, Melanija Knavs was "flat as a board," with no real bosom, luckily, however, this was just the time when traditional sexy curves were becoming less and less of a condition for a modeling career, as the designers in the 1990s sought out thin girls rather than full-figured ones, hangers, so to speak, for their fashion creations. The required photographs did not need to be professional and could be shot with amateur cameras, as long as the quality was sufficient. Most often these were taken by the applicant's friends, or the, to varying degrees jealous yet proud boyfriends, or morbidly ambitious parents, who saw in their daughters money-making supermodels and were already counting the dollars and deutschmarks.

Melanija Knavs never became a supermodel, she did, however – when it comes to counting dollars – become by far the richest Slovenian on the planet. Back in 1992, when Amalija and Viktor Knavs sent their youngest daughter to compete in the first Slovenian Look of the Year contest, they could not have imagined anything even remotely close in their wildest dreams.

Chapter 6

A STAR IS BORN

Petar Radović was nervously looking for Stojan Auer all over the Grand Hotel Emona in Bernardin near Portorož. He was nowhere to be found. Then Auer's wife Karmen suggested he checked their hotel room. Nearly panicking by this point, Radović indeed rushed up to the room and, sure enough, Auer was still there, even though the grand opening of Saturday's live broadcast of the first Slovenian Look of the Year contest on TV Slovenija's "Channel 1" was minutes, not hours away. But Stojan Auer had come down with diarrhea and was barely able to leave his hotel room. He was falling to pieces with stage fright, as this was his first big appearance on Slovenian national television. Until then he had only worked for TV Slovenija's regional branch in Maribor, where he hosted local entertainment programs, including quiz shows.

The studio in Maribor where Stojan Auer began his successful television career had been run for years by Janez Ujčič, a legendary TV producer who went on to co-found Pop TV, today Slovenia's most successful commercial television channel, owned by America Central Media Enterprises, or Time Warner.

After selling his shares of Pro Plus to the television corporation that broadcasts Pop TV and Kanal A, Ujčič founded the Maribor regional TV station Tele 59, which, after the megalomaniac purchase of its studio, the building of the former Kino Union cinema, ended up going bankrupt to the tune of several million dollars. At the end of his career Ujčič even turned to politics, rising high in the ranks of the Democratic Party of Pensioners of Slovenia, and was even State Secretary at the Ministry of Culture during Prime Minister Janez Janša's government. In 2016 the retired television mogul and former politician Janez Ujčič declared personal bankruptcy.

Ujčič had been known as a bit of a playboy and a car enthusiast during his active career, particularly fond of Audis. One of his most notorious trophy women was the television host Katja Tratnik.

But before the freshly powdered Look of the Year caravan headed off to the Slovenian coast on 11 June 1992, the official semi-finals were held in Gradišče (now known by its older name Sveta Trojica), a romantic village nestled in the gently rolling hills of Slovenian Styria, much closer to Sevnica, Melanija Knavs' hometown, than Portorož. The location chosen for the semi-finals was an inn owned by Srečko Vogrin, a relative of the later infamous Ivan Vogrin, Mayor of the Municipality of Lenart and Member of Slovenian Parliament, who was convicted of improper practices and accumulating debts in his bankrupt private company, which sold windows.

The editor-in-chief of *Jana*, Bernarda Jelkin, known as "The Red Baroness," was in a patriotic mood. She was first called Red Baroness by the famous and now late Slovenian journalist and editor Danilo Slivnik, because of the refined way she edited two magazines, *Jana* and the tabloid *Lady*, according to media guidelines of Communist politics, especially those of President Milan Kučan, Slivnik committed suicide in January 2012. A few days after the semifinals in an op-ed piece in the magazine Jana Jelkin wrote that *"The semifinals should show that an independent Slovenia can bring an astounding number of radiant faces and figures to the international modeling scene.... Normally competitions select one or two really interesting faces who can reach the top, with all the rest trailing behind."*

Bernarda Jeklin, who liked to brag about how she went for a coffee with Milan Kučan when he was still president of the Communist Party and later of the country before her editorial meetings at *Jana* magazine, publicly showed her strong political affiliation in 2008, when she actively joined the political party Zares, led by former Secretary-General of the party Liberal Democracy of Slovenia, Gregor Golobič.

It is said that at the event in Gradišče out of the 43 semifinalists chosen from the over 200 applicants (not bad for a country of only two million citizens), it was hard to find a bad candidate. Bernarda Jeklin, for one, was convinced as much. Though she was at first glance just the first dame of the Slovenian tabloid scene, she was actually an experienced and calculating master of mass media manipulation.

The international jury, in which the final word was given to Andrea Weidler, owner of Wiener Modellsekretariat, and Jurij Maleševič, head of Interdesign, who was also the president of the jury, had a hard job. In the end they whittled the competition down to 12 girls who, in Jelkin's words, *"seemed to stand out for their radiance."* Among them, of course, were the eventual grand-prize winner Martina Kajfež, as well as runner-ups Mojca Mladenovič and the future Melania Trump.

One or two girls were just a half an inch or so too short to make it to the final. This might seem a preposterous margin to preclude success, but under the strict eyes of the experts in the jury, half an inch can deal the fatal blow.

Ultimately though, as fashion history later showed, Bernarda Jeklin, who at the time confidently strolled around Portorož with her golden retriever, was wrong. None of the three up-and-coming Slovenian models who celebrated their victory that day in Portorož reached the peak of the world of haute couture as Jeklin had predicted. None became supermodels, and none ever reached the ranks of the likes of Claudia Schiffer, Cindy Crawford, Kate Moss, or Christy Turlington.

Martina Kajfež, as fashion managers discovered, was way too stubborn for the business, and her father meddled too much in her business affairs. Mojca Mladenovič on the other hand came off as slightly strange. As for Melanija Knavs, well, we all know that she found wealth and success in a different way, after meeting Donald Trump through Italian fashion agent Paolo Zampolli.

In Gradišče in Styria, not far from the Austrian border, things got off to a true Hollywood start, at least by

Slovenian standards. Andrea Weidler, the decisive owner of Wiener Modellsekretariat, who had herself been a famous model, even earning the moniker the Grande Dame of the Austrian fashion scene, pulled up at Srečko Vogrin's inn that evening in a huge limousine, one of those American cruisers. She was accompanied by Frano Lasić, a well known Croatian film, TV, and music star, known for his blond hair and charming demeanor. He is most known in Slovenia for his cult Yugoslav movie and TV show *Occupation in 26 Pictures*, by director Lordan Zafranović, as well as the hit song *Volim te budalo mala*. Lasić is a native of Dubrovnik, the stunningly beautiful historical city on the south Dalmatian coast in Croatia, the pearl in the Adriatic Sea that has gained renown as one of the main filming locations in HBO's hit series *Game of Thrones*. During the war of the 1990s Dubrovnik was bombed by the Yugoslavian army and Serbian and Montenegrin reservists; Lasić escaped in the nick of time to Vienna, later also arranging for his parents to join him.

Even before Lasić's parents left Dubrovnik, their old and beautiful patrician home had been hit by three Montenegrin mortar shells that almost demolished it. When Lasić was in Gradišče, his parents had already moved back to Dubrovnik, as the worst of the war was already over.

Frano Lasić also spent a few years in the United States, where he first traveled to in 1983, he then lived in England, before moving to Vienna where he became a business partner to Andrea Weidler, and the two were also quite close personally. While Lasić was abroad, he had completely disappeared from the Yugoslavian media scene. Being a member of the semi-final jury in the Look of the Year contest, along with some pictures in Jana, was something of a comeback for him.

When Ms. Weidler stepped out of her limousine in front of the inn in Gradišče, she took one look at the young women and exclaimed, *"Wunderbar, how many perfect girls there are!"* To a degree the fashion manager, known as a professionally quite decisive woman, was absolutely right. The locals at Gradišče will almost certainly never again see that many Slovenian beauties gathered in one spot.

Beside Andrea Weidler, three employees from the Milan-based R.V.R. also showed up in Gradišče, but the Parisians from the Metropolitan informed them that they would be showing up only at the finale in Portorož. Thus the Austrian Andrea Weidler and Croatian Frano Lasić remained the main stars of that evening in Gradišče, while Bernarda Jeklin boasted that, *"After what we have seen here in Gradišče, we have no anxiety over the finale at the Bernardin in Portorož. We are confident and convinced that despite this being our first time, nothing can go wrong. The reason for this is that we are surrounded by so much noble Slovenian beauty, ready and confident enough to take on the competition on European catwalks."*

Among the stars at the semi-finals in Gradišče was the event's host, Stojan Auer. He knew that Gradišče was merely an introduction to the event in Portorož, his long awaited move from local TV that would launch his career on the national stage. Stojan Auer's media, professional, and political career could have sounded like a true American success story had he not along the way become embroiled in criminal activities for which he was convicted and spent some time in jail.

His hit show on the local TV channel in Maribor *Poglej in Zadeni* (See and Win) hit the big time in 1992 when it moved to the national broadcaster TV Slovenija in a prime-time slot. On the show he hosted many guests of global renown, which, for a country that had just opened its borders only a year before, was a phenomenal media achievement. Up to that point, and even since, no other Slovenian TV host had succeeded in doing this, despite the fact that Slovenia joined the European Union just a few years later.

Poglej in Zadeni was broadcast on TV Slovenija for 5 years. When the relationship between Auer and TV Slovenija soured, he moved on to Pop TV, but his new show called *Super Pop*, was not nearly as successful, marking the relatively quick end of his TV career after that.

When Auer stopped hosting shows on TV Slovenija and Pop TV, he remained in media as the owner of local Maribor radio station Radio Net FM as well as the TV station Net TV. He also became the owner of the large, multi-purpose venue called Lent on the banks of the Drava River, one of central Europe's largest and longest rivers, flowing from the Dolomites in northeastern Italy, through Austria, past Maribor in Slovenia, finally discharging into the Danube at the Croatian city of Osijek.

In 2005, however, Stojan Auer was convicted of tax evasion after illegally acquiring 25.5 million Slovenian tolars (around $120,000) and was sentenced to a year in prison. With no recourse to appeal he was forced, a year later, to spend time in prison in Rogoza near Maribor, but he was soon released after the sentence was overturned. A rather portly lawyer from Maribor, Stanka Gavez Firm, who had formerly been a judge at the same court that sentenced Auer, worked hard to gain his release, and even a Committee for Supporting Stojan Auer was created. Even though the case was soon overturned by the Supreme Court and Auer was released, the scandal was a huge blow professionally and he never really recovered as a businessman, or a media mogul. He soon lost his ownership of Net TV, which now struggles along with a paltry $35,000 in revenues per year, almost non-existent viewership and advertisement revenue. He did manage to keep his radio station and the large events hall at Lent.

Stojan Auer then, possibly also to protect the remnants of his business empire in the style of a kind of Maribor version of Silvio Berlusconi, passionately entered politics. He founded a local political party, the List for Justice and Development, a name he quite evidently and nonchalantly appropriated from the Movement for Justice and Development, founded by the late Slovenian President Janez Drnovšek at the zenith of his political career, after he was Prime Minister and President of the party Liberal Democrats of Slovenia. After Drnovšek's death, his Movement for Justice and Development, whose last leader was the former rector of the University of Ljubljana, Stane Pejovnik, fell apart and support for his party LDS under the leadership of Katarina Kresal also dropped dramatically and the party failed to get the necessary votes to even enter parliament in the 2011 elections.

As President of his List for Justice and Development, Stojan Auer unsuccessfully ran for Mayor of Maribor in 2010, and a year later ran for parliament, this time as a member of Janez Janša's right wing Slovenian Democratic Party. He failed to win a seat. Today the political clout of Auer's List – along with that of Auer himself – has drastically fallen. His political rivals now say that he is trying to use what remaining power he has in the Maribor political scene to maintain a certain measure of influence over Maribor-based companies under municipal ownership, thus ensuring that advertising money keeps coming into his radio station. Trying to keep costs down, he has even resorted to hosting and moderating most shows on his Radio FM Net.

Back then, though, right before the finale of the Look of the Year competition in June 1992, in which the future Mrs. Trump competed, Stojan Auer was right at the beginning of his fame and career. The man most responsible for Stojan Auer's success was probably Petar Radović, director and television personality from head to toe, who conquered Maribor and then the rest of Slovenia from neighboring Croatia.

The director Petar Radović, who in the 1980s made his fame on Croatian national television HTV where he worked with legendary editor and journalist Silvije Hum, was invited to Slovenia by Dare Hering, later a member of the singing group New Swing Quartet under directorship of popular singer Oto Pestner. The New Swing Quartet is one of the few successful groups in Slovenia that sings soul music. Radović, who had grown tired of the routine of directing broadcasts from Split and other Croatian music festivals for Zagreb TV, first approached Lado Ambrožič, who was at the time news editor of news at TV Slovenija. Ambrožič told him straight up that there was no work for him on the news, sending him instead to Janez Ujčič in Maribor. Ujčič immediately offered him the task of directing Stojan Auer's show *Poglej in Zadeni*. This was the start of a long and fruitful television partnership between Stojan Auer and Petar Radović. The two TV partners, despite their common course, were very different in at least two ways; to start with, Peter Radović was never connected to scandals and speculations about what was happening with the money that *Poglej in Zadeni* brought in after it switched to a national format. At the very center of the scandal were Stojan Auer and Janez Lombergar, the long time director of TV Slovenija, who was said to have used the money from production and selling advertisement time on *Poglej in Zadeni* to build himself a villa by the Slovenian coast, in the region known as the Slovenian Provence.

There was never enough evidence to support the allegations against Stojan Auer and Janez Lombergar, especially as the production was partially financed with taxpayers' money through RTV Slovenija's federal funding, so they remained rumors and cautious media observations. It is true, however, that at some point that management at RTV Slovenija suddenly decided to pull the plug on the production and broadcasts of *Poglej in Zadeni*, which many in the media connected to the alleged controversial financial flows in connection with the show. Today Petar Radović lives in a two-bedroom apartment in Vič, an urban neighborhood in southern Ljubljana.

Another big difference between Petar Radović and Stojan Auer was their approach to women. Radović, a well-known playboy, married four times, today lives with Vesna Perona, a producer at TV Slovenija that he met on Pop TV. Auer, on the other hand, has been with his wife Karmen the whole time, and she doubles as his business secretary. More widespread than the rumors that Auer cheated on his wife with countless beauties from the Slovenian entertainment scene, never with any specific names, was the suggestion that Auer is gay.

A few weeks before Martina Kajfež, Mojca Mladenovič, Melanija Knavs, and other finalists in the Look of the Year competition headed off to Portorož for the finale, *Jana* published a rare article about Donald Trump. It reported that the then 41-year old billionaire was the richest man on Earth, and that he was building the tallest skyscraper in the world on the Hudson river in New York, towering with its 150 stories over 1800 feet above the ground, making it the tallest building yet, and the previous record holder, the Sears Tower in Chicago with its modest 1450 feet, look short by comparison. The American magazine *Fortune* estimated Trump's wealth at $1.3 billion, claiming that Trump is becoming richer by about $2 million a day, every day.

For his former wife Ivana Trump, who was at one point even vice-president of the Trump business empire and whose annual salary amounted to a symbolic single dollar, Donald Trump bought the old Plaza Hotel on the edge of

Her first cover: Melanija in *Jana* (photo: Dean Dubokovič, *Jana*, June 1992).

Dinner at Lake Bled, July 2002 – from left: father Viktor, Norma Foerderer, mother Amalija, Melania, Donald Trump, and Dušan Furar (photo: Alenka Žavbi – Dušan Furar's personal files).

"Trump's" table at the restaurant Julijana in the Grand Hotel Toplice, Bled (authors' documentation).

Bled and its surroundings, *A piece of Paradise*, as claimed by the Slovenian poet Prešeren. (photo: Jošt Gantar, www.jostgantar.com).

The crystal crib sent as a gift to the Trumps by the Rogaška Slatina glassworks (authors' documentation).

Donald and Melania Trump talk to a crowd of voters in Cedar Rapids on the day of the Iowa Caucus (photo: Profimedia; February 2016).

Melania at the Republican Presidential Debate on CNBC in Boulder, Colorado (photo: Profimedia, October 2015).

Donald and Melania Trump announce his run for the Presidency at Trump Tower in New York (photo: Profimedia, June 2015).

Lara, Eric, Melania, Barron, Donald, Ivanka, and Donald Trump Jr. attending The Celebrity Apprentice season finale at Trump Tower in New York City (photo: Profimedia, February 2015).

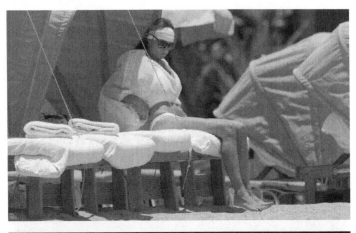

Melania in a see-through white sun dress wearing a bikini and enjoying her vacation with her son Barron in Hawaii (photo: Profimedia, July 2013).

Melania promotes hew new skincare line at Trump Tower. She is wearing a creation by Victoria Beckham (photo: Profimedia, April 2013).

Melania, Donald, and Barron Trump at the Trump Invitational Grand Prix, Mar-a-Lago in Palm Beach, Florida (photo: Profimedia, January 2013).

Donald and Melania Trump at the US Open Men's Final, Billie Jean King National Tennis Center in NYC (photo: Profimedia, September 2011).

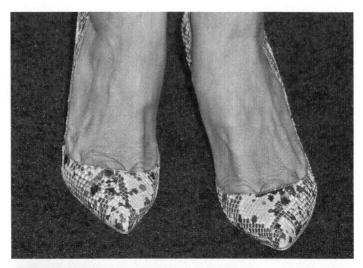

Melania in tight shoes attends the New York premiere of *The Dark Knight Rises* held at AMC Lincoln Square Theatre (photo: Profimedia, July 2012).

Beyoncé, Solange, Donald, and Melania Trump, Amber Heard, Brooke Shields, Matthew Morrison, Gary Oldman, and Zac Posen seen leaving the Metropolitan Museum of Art's Costume Institute Gala in Manhattan (photo: Profimedia, May 2012).

Melania with her new QVC jewelry line in her home office at Trump Residential at 721 5th Avenue (photo: Profimedia, July 2011).

The frowning Melania at the inauguration mass of Governor-Elect Chris
Christie and Lieutenant Governor-Elect Kim Guadagno held at the Cathedral
Basilica of the Sacred Heart Newark (photo: Profimedia, January 2010).

Melania and her mother Amalija take Barron for a stroll down Madison Avenue in New York City (photo: Profimedia, October 2007).

Melania and her son Barron by the Donald Trump Walk of Fame Ceremony held in front of the Kodak Theatre (photo: Profimedia, January 2007).

First shots of the pregnant Melania and Donald Trump at Shaquille O'Neal's 33rd birthday celebration party at the Hotel Victor in Miami Beach (photo: Profimedia, March 2005).

Melania and Donald Trump giving an interview after the Republican presidential candidates debate at the Fox Theater in Detroit (photo: Profimedia, March 2016).

A visor with a badge with Melania Trump posing in front of the Stars and Stripes and the words *America's Next First Lady* written on it, worn by a Trump supporter in Kansas City, Missouri (photo: Profimedia, March 2016).

Central Park, coughing up a good $390 million. The sum of one dollar as an annual salary was not the invention of Donald and Ivana Trump, as the one-dollar salary club has other prominent members like Lee Iacocca from Chrysler, Michael Bloomberg while he was Mayor of New York, John F. Kennedy as the President of the United States, and Mark Zuckerberg at the helm of Facebook.

At the time, Trump said that he would never want to be President of the Unites States, as he would have to move to the White House, which was much smaller than his apartment. He lived with Ivana and three children in Trump Tower, in an apartment with 21,000 square feet of livable space, heading off to a 46-room house in Connecticut at weekends. In winter they usually took their private Boeing 727 to Florida to the Mar-a-Lago estate in Palm Beach with its 110 rooms and lavish grounds.

This mansion at Mar-a Lago, however, was not built by Donald Trump or his father Fred Trump, who in Queens alone owned 23,000 apartments, but by Marjorie Merriweather Post, heiress to the Cornflakes fortune, back in 1927. It was built and decorated by the best architects and designers used by European royalty.

Two weeks before the magazine *Jana* also published a much shorter article about Donald Trump, in which an anonymous author claimed that Trump's Czech wife Ivana, as soon as Trump had sent her away, had immediately taken up with a good-looking Italian, evoking a slew of comments from the media. After receiving this blow to his reputation, he tried to get back into the media's good graces, promoting a picture of him handing over a $30,000 check to Mother

Hale, the famed 87-year old social worker. The money was intended for children infected with HIV.

Today, Trump's net worth is estimated to be around 10 billion US dollars or 9.15 billion euros. As the Republican candidate for the President of the United States he declared an income of 557 million US dollars in 2015 to the Federal Election Committee (FEC).

The Bernardin hotel complex, which in June 1992 was completely owned by the state, and which today is a part of the semi-public company Sava Turizem and the target of tycoon squabbles for former state assets, was built in one of the prettiest spots along the barely 26-mile-long Slovenian coast, between the historical city of Piran and the more modern resort of Portorož, which the tourism industry has for years unsuccessfully been trying to turn into the Slovenian Monte Carlo. Locals and people who follow the local situation in Piran and Portorož have found, much to their ire, that both towns have recently fallen under the influence of the Albanian mafia, who among other things might be responsible for the suicide of the well-known restaurateur Mladen Škerbec, friend of numerous prominent people from the Slovenian showbusiness scene. The unfortunate Škerbec allegedly gave up under mafia pressure surrounding financial debts that he had racked up by gambling. His suicide is also said to have been nonchalantly investigated, with the Albanian mafia even has a good part of Piran's criminal investigators under its control.

The headland in front of the hotel where the Look of the Year competition took place is dominated by the medieval church of St. Bernardine. It is a popular venue for weddings for famous and less famous Slovenes.

Honorary guests of the event had already begun arriving, and the most attention was generated by the young Slovenian politician Marjan Podobnik and the notorious Milan-based Croatian photographer Čedo Komljenović.

Marjan Podobnik, leader of the Slovenian People's Party, and later Deputy Prime Minister in Janez Drnovšek's coalition government with Drnovšek's Liberal Democracy of Slovenia, drove himself to the event from his hometown of Cerkno, along with his wife Tatjana Podobnik, daughter of the farmer and politician Ivan Oman, member of the first government after Slovenia's independence and founder of the Slovene Rural Association, which later transformed into the Slovenian People's Party. At the time politics was Podobnik's entire life, making it not unusual that he drove straight home after the Look of the Year finals to get a couple hours of sleep before setting off again before sunrise the following morning to attend a political gathering in Murska Sobota, a few hour's drive away, right on the other side of the country.

After the end of his political career, Marjan Podobnik was also briefly Chairman of the Management Board of Telekom Slovenije, and then tried his hand at chicken farming in Serbia. It was unsuccessful and the failed venture earned him a great deal of laughs from Slovenian media. Today he is still held to be influential behind the scenes of the Slovenian People's Party, and as a politician from the shadows tends to raise his voice whenever the issue of the fiercely contested – and still undefined – coastal border between Slovenia and Croatia comes up.

Marjan's older brother Janez Podobnik, a doctor by profession, was also President of the Slovenian People's Party, as well as Speaker of Slovenian Parliament and Minister of the Environment, and today works as a consultant for gaining EU funds for business ventures related to environmental protection.

For the fashion world and for Melanija Knavs, the photographer Čedo Komljenović was an more important guest than Marjan Podobnik. He was one of the best known Yugoslavian names in the European jet set and his photographic agency was one of Italy's most exclusive. He was a cult photographer in Croatia, often using the nome de plume Monty Shadow. Komljenović was also known for introducing Miss Croatia Slavica Malić to Formula 1 founder Bernie Ecclestone. Her marriage to Bernie, for years one of the wealthiest men in Britain, made Slavica Ecclestone the richest Croatian, just as marrying Donald Trump made Melanija Knavs the richest Slovenian, with the difference that Slavica and Bernie eventually divorced.

Čedo Komljenović was the subject of numerous rumors, that he was in fact more or less a high-society pimp, introducing beautiful, ambitious girls to global stars. Take the Slovenian beauty Nataša Dobelšek, for instance, who lived in Italy and tried with Čedo's help to forge a modeling career, who he introduced to Hollywood actor and his friend Sylvester Stallone. Nataša Dobelšek soon returned home without a successful international modeling career. All she has to show for it are a few parties and photos with Komljenović, Stallone, and other stars, though only to the most naive and kind tabloid journalists gave her any attention. On the Slovenian scene she was helped by journalist and comedian Tone Fornezzi-Tof, known himself for appreciating beautiful girls. There was also talk of him, for as long as he could, requesting 'commission' in bodily pleasures from the ambitious belles he was supposedly helping along in their career.

When Melanija Knavs arrived in Portorož, she had already accumulated quite some experience as a model, not just the test shots at Stane Jerko's studio in January of 1987.

In the summer of 1977, almost ten years before Stane Jerko discovered her, as a seven-year old girl from Sevnica she appeared, together with her friends Nena Bedek and Diana Kosar, in a fashion show for Mura and Jutranjka in Radenci. Melanija, Nena, and Diana of course wore clothes from the socialist Jutranjka factory, where their mothers worked. That same summer Melanija shot two sessions for Jutranjka, the pictures from which were published in the well-known, now defunct magazine *Maneken*.

Maneken published pictures of the child model Melanija also in 1978, when Melanija did some work for the Croatian firm Tekstilni Kombinat from Zagreb, a year later for Vezenine Bled, and in 1980 for Novoteks from Novo Mesto. It is not known whether Viktor and Amalija Knavs received payment for the modeling work their daughter Melanija, and occasionally Ines, did. Probably not, as the norm at the time was that compensation was arranged in kind, namely in the form of clothes and accessories from those companies advertised in the fashion shows or photo shoots.

Two years after Melanija Knavs was "discovered" by Stane Jerko, she once again appeared in *Maneken* wearing clothes for Alpina, Šešir, Kroj, and Pletenje, for their respective fall and winter collections for the 1988/1989 season. This was also to be the last issue of *Maneken*.

The same year, 1989, Melanija Knavs went to Rome, where she won a beauty contest to appear in movies for Cinecittà Roma. Interestingly, though, her victory in the Italian capital did nor lead to any major engagements in Italy or elsewhere, and, no need to mention, it never lead anything close to an acting contract. Nothing at all.

Probably extremely disappointed, as she was a very ambitious young woman who desperately wanted a modeling career, Melanija returned to Ljubljana and took part in the traditional fashion trade fair at the Ljubljana Exhibition and Convention Center.

Melanija never appeared much in the media. The Ljubljana-based magazine *Stop*, which focused on TV, movies, and music, published a group photo of the creative team behind the Studio Moda clip for *Studio City*, where Melanija had played the American President, but not because of Melanija, rather because of the show's host Jožica Brodarič and director Andrej Košak. Melanija Knavs, though an ambitious model, was completely unknown to the media at this point, and the tabloids had not even heard of her. Even the photographer Stane Jerko only began talking to journalists about her after she had become Donald Trump's escort. Before that no journalist had ever even asked him about Melanija Knavs.

The Look of the Year competition for *Jana* was thus the first opportunity of its kind for Melanija to make it into the media. At the time, in Communist Slovenia, tabloids as such did not really exist, except in part for *Stop, Jana,* and *Antena,* which were more or less marketed at teenagers, and the only just emerging magazine *Lady*. In most fashion circles, the only exposure Melanija had got at the time, though she definitely was not famous, was through her TV commercial for Subrina shampoo.

Melanija accordingly hedged all her hopes on winning in Portorož on 11 to 13 June 1992. But the crown here went to the favorite, the brunette with full lips and bosom, Martina Kajfež from Nova Gorica, a town that was built on the order of Tito after WWII on the Yugoslavian side of the border with Italy, as a communist counterpart to the Italian city of Gorizia, which after the Treaty of Paris the Allies ceded to Italy despite it having been liberated by Yugoslavian partisans and the Yugoslavian side claiming it as their own.

Martina Kajfež was eighteen at the time, four years Melanija's junior, and was *"tall as a mountain"* and *"skinny as a birch tree,"* with a proud and defiant face, sensual lips and features that harked to a Slovenian mix between the actress Rita Hayworth and the supermodel Claudia Schiffer, as the more sophisticated male spectators at the Look of the Year finale established. It was probably no coincidence that Martina Kajfež was put on the cover of Jana right before the final, although the magazine's editors later apologized, saying it was purely a chance occurrence.

Martina Kajfež had just finished the fourth year of a five-year high school for design, specifically architecture and interior design, in the Italian Gorizia, as was completely fluent in Italian. She had intended on applying to the Academy of Fine Arts in Venice that fall, where the entry requirements included just 3 years at a design school and qualifications for teaching fine arts, which Martina had already studied for in Gorica. So Martina followed a similar path to Ines and Melanija, only that she did not apply to the school in Ljubljana, as her parents, Jolanda and Andrej, a dentist who, according to many agents, later got far too involved in his daughter's career, the Slovenian capital was way too far away from Nova Gorica.

Unlike Mojca Mladenovič and Melanija Knavs, Martina Kajfež had no experience in modeling before the Look of the Year competition. This was why she was convinced that Mojca or Melanija would win, especially Mojca who, *"had mastered all the secrets of modeling,"* as she explained to journalists after her victory. Her first time in front of a camera, in fact, was just weeks before Look of the Year got started, when a friend told Martina's mother Jolanda, then employed at Nova Gorica's radio station, about the competition, and then arranged for test shots with Stane Jerko. They sent these pictures to the competition's organizers just two weeks before the start of the competition and the semi-final in Gradišče was the first time she had ever posed in her life.

To ensure she was ready for the competition and that she would improvise as little as possible in Portorož, Kajfež practiced poses in front of a mirror at home, but she had very little time, as the competition happened to be during the week of her end of year exams.

She knew she was beautiful. At the age of fourteen she began noticing that people in the street turned their heads when she passed them, and friends tried to persuade her mother to push her daughter into a modeling career. It became clear to her that she was no ugly duckling, that the people looking at her on the streets were doing so because she was beautiful, not because she was ugly. Martina, however, was rather self-critical, *"I'm not a great beauty, even though I may have a nice body, my face is anything but pretty. It is trendy, at least everyone tells me, to have blue eyes and full lips."*

There was one thing that set Kajfež apart from her peers, though; she was a motocross rider, usually at weekends. She had even been seriously considering seriously pursuing this sport, but then realized that the scratched and bruised legs she got from motocross would not really go hand-in-hand with modeling.

She was an only child. At first this made her feel sad, but she later, when she saw the siblings some get into, thought it was better this way.

Martina Kajfež was late to the dress rehearsal for the final, then *Jana* VIP guests saw her running past reception along the path that today joins the Grand Hotel Bernardin with the rest of the complex. She was sporting huge curlers in her hair, the product of the Trieste-based hair salon Famiglia Artistica. Desperate and lost she was a whole hour late to the rehearsal, but five hours later she stood on the stage as winner, with a bouquet of flowers and a radiant smile that reflected happiness as much as surprise. She knew that after that night in Portorož her life would change.

True enough; the jury changed her life forever. The decision had come from the representatives from Paris, Vienna, and Milan, namely Maja Draženović from the Metropolitan, Andrea Weidler from Modellsekretariat, and Pier-Carlo Borgogelli from R.V.R. Reclame, as well as in part Slovenia's most influential fashion agent Marina Masowietsky, while jury member Bernarda Jeklin was less decisive in the result. After winning, Martina knew it was time to say goodbye to mom's cooking, playing with her Schnauzer named Giorgio, and motocross racing, as the time had come to sign a contract with the Parisian Metropolitan, which was to clear the way for her to the catwalks of Paris, London, Munich, and more, at least for the following three years.

Andrej Kajfež, the big winner's father, was bursting with joy. When photographers came to take Martina Kajfež's pictures on the hotel's terrace in every conceivable pose, shouting at her, *"Come on, Martina, breathe some life into your face. Think what you want to express, do you want to be aggressive, natural, romantic, cute,"* Andrej Kajfež explained to reporters that, *"our Martina is living the dream of many women, but she barely realizes it."*

A few years later the fashion agent Wolfgang Schwarz, among other things the author of *Sold Beauty: An Inside Report on the World of the Beautiful and Rich*, accused Andrej Kajfež of getting too involved in her affairs and being pathologically overprotective, preventing her from becoming a top model.

Nonetheless, Schwarz was more interested in Martina Kajfež than in Melanija Knavs. With her first place Kajfež got a three-year contract with Metropolitan, her modeling career only had limited success. She was, in Schwarz's opinion, too stubborn to achieve the status of top model. Martina moved to Italy with her mother Jolanda, and now, aged 42, lives in Sicily. Every so often she makes a commercial in Slovenia, lastly for the jewelers Zlatarna Celje, and she is also a wedding photographer.

Shortly after winning in Portorož, Martina Kajfež spent time dating the popular Slovenian singer Jan Plestenjak until she dropped him, apparently also due to his mother Dora Plestenjak, a well-known painter, constantly interfering in their relationship.

A few years later Dora Plestenjak was accused by the police, the Center for Social Work, and other authorities of sexually abusing her grandchild, the son of Jan's half-brother Domen Slana and his former wife, Janja Ošlaj. The trial was held in courts both in Ljubljana and Kranj, but in secrecy, in the interest of protecting personal information and for the benefit of a minor. She was ultimately acquitted, but rumor has it that mostly due to her ties with politicians and judges, with not little help from the state prosecutor and later Minister of Justice and vice-president of the Liberal Democratic Party, Zdenka Cerar, the late mother of the current Slovenian Prime Minister Miro Cerar. When Janja Ošlaj, who had brought suit against Dora Plestenjak, complained to Human Rights Ombudsman Matjaž Hanžek over the case's dismissal, the responding comment was that there was little they could do, this is a *"small country, influential family."* Hanžek is today a Member of Parliament with the radical leftist party United Left, dubbed the Slovenian Syriza, under the leadership of the young political demagogue Luka Mesec.

When in September 2005 the co-author of this book Bojan Požar, as editor-in-chief of the paper *Direkt*, published news of the until then hushed up story about the charges against Dora Plestenjak, the court in Ljubljana sentenced him to a three-month conditional prison sentence, which briefly silenced any reporting on sexual abuse of children in the social elite of Slovenia. Domen Slana also later got embroiled in a law suit over alleged defamation, claiming that his former wife Janja Ošlaj got a design job with the oil-derivatives company Petrol by sleeping with its CEO Franci Perčič, later an influential advisor to the Slovenian President Danilo Türk.

Martina Kajfež and Melanija Knavs, or rather Melania Trump, are not in contact today.

Melanija Knavs shared second place on the winners' podium of the Look of the Year contest with Mojca Mladenovič from Ljubljana. Like Melanija, Mojca was not inexperienced when it came to modeling, although, at the tender age of sixteen, she was a whole six years younger than Melanija. Mojca Mladenovič also attended the Secondary School for Design in Ljubljana where she chose the course in industrial design, and in Portorož she was looked after by her mother and father.

Director and playboy Petar Radović even publicly complained that it had been *"practically impossible to get to the girls"* in Portorož since it was not only parents who kept an eye over their daughters, but also the chief dames of the competition, Marina Masowietsky, Bernarda Jeklin, and Vera Hegeduš, a stylist and in the 1970s the notorious owner of Veronika, one of the first fashion boutiques in communist Slovenia. They just did not let anyone close, according to Radović.

It is spoken in the alleys of Ljubljana that Vera Hegeduš, who later founded the company Image Management, burnt down her own boutique to cash in on the insurance money and then dedicated herself to managing models and fashion publishing. With her daughter, the model Tea Hegeduš, she began publishing the magazine *Glamour*, followed by *Lepota* (Beauty) and *Gloss*. Today Vera Hegeduš is once again a stylist at Maxi, a high-end department store in the heart of Ljubljana. Maxi is now owned by Mercator, which was recently acquired by the richest man in Croatia and owner of Agrokor, Ivica Todorić.

Hegeduš, who outwardly always appeared nervous and hostile, decked out and done up like a typical Ljubljana boutique socialite, liked to boast to the media how she wakes up at seven how from nine o'clock the phones just don't stop ringing as she works journeying between Ljubljana and the Croatian capital Zagreb until 1 or 2 in the morning.

Mojca Mladenovič began her modeling career out of sheer curiosity. She once answered an advertisement from the Slovenian fashion agency Zoom Promotion, took a modeling class, and then did some a few shots for fashion magazines. Then, in 1991, she was spotted, quite by chance,

at Ljubljana Castle by someone working for Wiener Modellsekretariat and she began modeling for the Austrians.

She was also a keen jazz ballet dancer tutored by the
well-known Ljubljana choreographer Mojca Horvat, and
she also competed in step. Indeed she was national step
champion, along with her friend Tina Tome. Mojca brought
this title to the renowned Ljubljana dance school Urška,
which closed down a year ago, after the death of its legendary founder Tomaž Ambrož and co-owners and Ambrož's
heirs not being able to sort out their differences. Two years
ago Mojca Mladenovič started teaching step at Dansa, another dance school in Ljubljana.

Just as Martina Kajfež and Melanija Knavs are no
longer in contact, neither are Melanija Knavs and Mojca
Mladenovič. Kajfež and Mladenovič, however, became good
friends, and even spent some time together in Vienna.

Melanija Knavs was bitterly disappointed when the four
years younger Martina Kajfež was pronounced the winner
of the first Slovenian Look of the Year,. Though she hid well
behind the mask of the cool girl from Sevnica, people close
to her knew what was going on in her head. This was, after
all, the second big defeat in her career. She had won the
Cinecittà Roma beauty contest, but hadn't received any film
offers, and here she was in Portorož sharing the runner-up
spot. Martina Kajfež had stolen the spotlight from her, everything in Portorož that night had revolved around the girl
from Nova Gorica.

Nonetheless, a few days after Portorož Melanija Knavs
traveled to Milan, where she had been invited as the third-
placed winner to R.V.R. Reclame, but by August of the same

year she had already returned to Ljubljana and Sevnica. She later remembered Milan, the capita of fashion and northern Italy, as long hours of posing for photographers where *"the money I made as a model was not even enough to survive."* About modeling itself she said how *"it all seems like a fun and attractive merry-go-round, but I am quite aware that when the merry-go-round stops, will need to get back to study and work."*

Besides Martina Kajfež, Mojca Mladenovič, Melanija Knavs, and Alenka Ružič, the competition in Portorož launched another name to fame. This was Vesna Dolenc from Maribor, later notorious on both the Slovenian social and political scene The blonde beauty with a heavy, typical accent from her native region of Štajerska, never had a huge modeling career, but she did host several television shows and then later married the nine years younger Jure Janković, youngest son of the director of the largest Slovenian company, Mercator, as well as Mayor of Ljubljana and ill-fated candidate for Prime Minister, Zoran Janković, who is otherwise of Serbian roots. Even the huge wedding, at least by Slovenian standards, at the Habakuk hotel at the foot of the mountain Pohorje on the outskirts of Maribor, was a party in true Serbian fashion. The guests brought the newlyweds fancy gifts, and part of the wedding was said to be paid for by Mercator's business partners, even though the company was still under state ownership at the time.

Before Jure Janković, Vesna was married to the businessman Primož Ogrizek, though they split up when their joint company Vepri went completely bankrupt. Vesna opted for a swift divorce, and Primož fled to Serbia for a few years, while their debts were paid by Primož's forlorn parents, who were forced to take out a loan.

The relationship between Vesna Dolenc and Jure Janković was quite public, and heavily exploited by the media, mostly due to the controversial role that the Janković family plays in Slovenian politics and business. Jure Janković, his older brother Damijan, and their father Zoran were all investigated by a special parliamentary commission, and all three were under the magnifying glass of criminal investigators; Zoran Janković even underwent a special investigation from the state Commission for the Prevention of Corruption. Some procedures are still unfolding in the courts, and Zoran Janković remains the only Slovenian politician to have won fairly and squarely the parliamentary elections yet was unable to fulfill his mandate of forming a coalition government, due to his personal arrogance and dictatorial stance.

Janković has been compared in some aspects to the former Italian Prime Minister Silvio Berlusconi, and there is definitely something Trump-like in him too. You could put it the other way round, perhaps the silent majority of Americans want a president like Zoran Janković! Vesna Dolenc, who has kept the surname Janković, today lives with the former politician and deputy mayor of Ljubljana Slavko Slak.

The same year Melanija Knavs came third in the Slovenian Look of the Year competition, 1992, Ivana and Donald Trump got divorced. In the settlement Ivana got $20 million in cash, $14 million in real estate in Connecticut, $5 million from rentals on Trump's real estate, a yearly annuity of

$350,000, all the jewelry Trump had bought her, and 49% of the family estate Mar-a-Lago in Florida, which also functions as a club for elite society in Palm Beach.

Chapter 7

I AM MELANIJA,
I COME FROM SLOVENIA

"I am Melanija Knavs, I come from Slovenia."

These were the words the future Mrs. Trump uttered in broken English in the spring of 1993 when she knocked on the door at Naglergasse 25/3 in the center of Vienna. Sitting inside was Wolfgang Schwarz, the representative of the American Agency Elite for Europe and Asia, as well as the owner of Girls & Boys Agency Vienna.

Schwarz was, and still is, an important and influential name in the modeling industry, where there is a strict hierarchy, rather realistically depicted in the 2006 movie *The Devil Wears Prada*, where the award-winning actress Meryl Streep plays the legendary editor of the cult fashion magazine *Vogue*, Anna Wintour. Schwarz knew all about high hopes, ambitions, and also the dirty secrets of the fashion business and the world of the rich and beautiful.

Before setting up his own fashion agency, he was a successful model himself, in fact a pioneer in the business. He succeeded even as early as the 1980s in bringing world class supermodels such as Naomi Campbell, Linda Evangelista, and Nadja Auermann to Austria. In 2015 he wrote a book titled *Sold Beauty (Verkaufte Schönheit)*, published in German by the publishing house Echomedia Buch, where he gives an exclusive insider's perspective on what goes on in the fashion world with beautiful women living between money, power, sex, drugs, and rock and roll.

Melanija literally strolled up to his agency in Vienna, rang the doorbell, and waited at the door. She told him she had been sent by Marina Masowietsky, who was then the owner of the Slovenian model agency Interdesign, and explained that she wanted to work in Milan, Paris, and the States, but that since she had not had many offers there, she decided to try Vienna.

But Wolfgang Schwarz, who normally accommodated his up-and-coming young models in a special apartment, with six to nine living as flatmates, did not seem particularly interested in Melanija, even though he did arrange a few fashion jobs for her later on, including an ad for the Austrian airline Lauda Air. His focus in Slovenia was Martina Kajfež, though she soon proved a little to be too stubborn for his liking, and Schwarz was annoyed at her father interfering in her career. He remembers Andrej Kajfež as a man who was desperately jealous of his daughter.

Wolfgang Schwarz always used to say that it was not important that a girl was beautiful; what matters is a strong personality, ability and desire to work hard, too hard even, and an additional benefit is if the girl already knows foreign languages. Everything else is teachable. But any future supermodel has to have that hidden something in her, which a good, experienced fashion agent or scout can sense and recognize immediately.

When it came to girls from eastern European, former communist countries, Schwarz had extreme reservations. This was mostly due to their predilection for partying over hard work. For them modeling meant fame and enough money to get by, while they saw their future in marrying a wealthy husband. For Wolfgang Schwarz this counted eastern European girls out of supermodel material.

Indeed, Charlotte Hays, columnist for the *New York Daily News*, *The New York Observer*, and *The Washington Times*, in her book *The Fortune Hunters, Dazzling Women and the Men they Married*, also ranks Melanija Knavs, named the Lady from Ljubljana, among the most notorious women for pursuing rich and famous men, in this case Donald Trump. Charlotte Hays published her book in 2007, two years after Melania and Trump's marriage, and she devoted most of chapter 9 to the former Ms. Knavs.

Serbians and Croatians have a great term for this type of woman, known throughout the Balkans, namely: *sponzoruša*, implying that they are looking merely for a sponsor, not a partner. Back then Melanija Knavs was hardly a *sponzoruša*, but, as Schwarz would say later, she had little to offer.

"She never put the necessary effort into modeling, she was too cold, quiet, and didn't radiate any energy. In front of clients who wanted her for photoshoots and on catwalks she never opened up and had no idea how to charm them, so they rarely picked her."

In the autumn of the same year, however, Melanija Knavs did some work in Milan at a fashion show for renowned designers Gucci and Valentino, and then at a show for Pino Lancetti.

Melanija seems to have also infuriated Wolfgang Schwarz at some point, *"Sorry, but she was so stupid. And all the time like a dead fish. It was really hard to work with her. Top model in EU? Please? No, never."*

Schwarz later also commented that, *"her English was terrible."* Indeed even today Melania Trump, who has been a naturalized US citizen for years, living in New York for even longer, still speaks English with a heavy Eastern European accent. Wikipedia, lists her as speaking French, Serbian, German, Italian and – Slovenian, something she boasted about herself in recent interviews in the American media during her husband's campaign to become the Republican presidential nominee.

Melanija Knavs' breakthrough onto the European fashion scene only came when she appeared on the cover of the Spanish magazine *Bazaar*, although this happened already after rumors began to spread within the industry that she was with Donald Trump. Wolfgang Schwarz also recalls a deal, although he is not entirely certain, with a tobacco company in Paris which hired her to do an ad. This was 1998, the year that Melanija, then already Melania Knauss, met Trump in New York. Select Slovenian journalists were also invited to the shoot in Paris at the expense of the company, among them Jožica Brodarič, a fashion reporter on Slovenian national TV. The company paid for everything, including Melania Knauss' fee, but the actual commercial with Melania in the main role was never brought out.

Nonetheless, Wolfgang Schwarz considers it to have been *"the biggest deal of her life,"* at least up to that point.

It is also true that Wolfgang Schwarz does not like Donald Trump. They have met three times, always on Trump's yacht, where he hosted models from Elite. On his yacht Trump is said to act vulgarly, treating women like pieces of meat without the basics of good manners.

Wolfgang Schwarz also used to come to Slovenia. In June 1994 he was the head of a jury to select the best Slovenian model of the year (Look of the Year), under sponsorship of Elite. Schwarz said at the time that, *"Slovenia is a small country, but it is huge in beauty."* Also on the jury was Martina Kajfež, who was working for Elite at the time.

The Slovenian media at that time were busy reporting on the marriage of Donald Trump and TV star and former Miss America and Miss Universe Marla Ann Maples, the Georgia native, whom he met skiing in Aspen, where Trump was at a New Year's party with his wife Ivana. Like Ivana, Marla Maples was a long-legged blonde with huge eyes and big breasts, but thirteen years her junior. The whole night the two cast scowls in the other's direction, weighing each other up.

The next day things blew up. All three were eating at Bonnie's, a prestigious and expensive restaurant in downtown Aspen. There was snow on the ground outside, but in the warmth of the restaurant the masks on both women soon came off.

"Pff, you and love," Marla taunted, *"I'm the one who loves him."*

Ivana, meanwhile, was getting white in her face. She played dumb for a while, unable to find the right words, but then the dam broke. Witnesses, famous guests who were sitting at neighboring tables, pretended they didn't see or hear anything, but were gloatingly amused with it all.

Donald Trump and Marla Maples had no idea what Ivana Trump was saying, as she began screaming in her native Czech, but then she reined herself back in and delivered Marla a clear message, *"Get your paws off Donald or I'll wring your neck."*

But it was too late for Ivana, and Donald Trump acted like a typical man. He stared at the tablecloth, traced random doodles with his nails on the white fabric, and then complained later that this scandal could hurt some of his business ventures. When he got back to New York, he immediately contacted his lawyers and financial advisors to start dividing the couple's assets.

The media at this point began giving him the nickname Goldfinger, as money was all that mattered to him, and he clearly sees marriage and divorce as a good or bad business transaction. For Trump, everything was business. Donald Trump and Marla Maples married in 1992, and divorced in 1999.

Wolfgang Schwarz was not the only fashion agent who was not particularly excited about Melania Trump, and who would not have bet much on her modeling career. Marina Masowietsky also did not have her in particular esteem, as she once even threw away Melanija Knavs' modeling book, convinced that nothing would come of her career.

And Marina Masowietsky, even though from the small, and in terms of fashion wholly irrelevant, Slovenia, where she had had some serious financial troubles, even going into bankruptcy before deftly opening up a new company and agency, was no ordinary fashion scout. Petar Radović was surprised when he arrived with Marina at the world finals of the Look of the Year competition on the Spanish island of Mallorca. He had been sent there by the head of RTV Slovenija, Janez Čadež, to see in person what fashion events at the global level were like, and Radović was thrilled to take him up on the opportunity, even though he was scared to death of flying. What surprised him was how many of the big fashion stars from the global scene Marina Masowietsky knew through Wolfgang Schwarz, exchanging hugs with John Casablancas, the late founder of Elite Model Management, with Linda Evagelista, and with the highest-paid male model in the history of high fashion, Marcus Schenkenberg.

Nonetheless, despite Schwarz and Masowietsky's opinion of her and the slow start to her career, Melanija Knavs, by then Melania Knauss, did often work abroad, mostly in Milan, Paris, and Madrid, and at least once at a fashion show in Düsseldorf, capital and economic hub of the German region of North Rhine-Westphalia. Her clients included Les Copains, Coveri, Mariella Burani, Pernas, Versus, and Ferre, working mostly as a catwalk model, as she was not as good at photo sessions. She clearly realized this herself, and she decided to specialize in being a catwalk model instead.

Melanija Knavs later told American media that she had signed her first modeling contract in Italy at the age of eighteen, which was not true. She only made it to the Italian fashion market, Milan in particular, after participating at the Slovenian Look of the Year competition in Portorož, that is in 1992, when she began working for R.V.R. Reclame, and later for Riccardo Gay and then Elite Milano, the Italian branch of New York's Elite Model Management. Wolfgang Schwarz did not officially take her on but he did help her get a few modeling jobs.

One of the most experienced fashion scouts in Milan, who has been working there for over 30 years but who requested anonymity in this book, remembers Melanija Knavs, whom he had met many times at various casting calls, in much the same way as his Viennese colleague Wolfgang Schwarz.

She was uncommunicative and withdrawn, though not unfriendly. Her body was great, she was always sleek, and her skin was wonderful. He also rated her measurements as *"number 1."*

But somehow it never worked out for her at casting calls; she lacked that tiny bit of charm needed to forge a connection with commissions or individual clients. Mastering communication and knowing how to pose so the photographers are satisfied with you are the sine qua non of photo sessions. Photographers have a hard time working with models who aren't relaxed, and the outcome is usually catastrophic.

As much as she remembers and judging from her career, Melanija Knavs quickly realized that she was not cut out for working on photo shoots, and Riccardo Gay's agency came to the same conclusion. Melanija said that she was not satisfied with the agency, whose headquarters were in a beautiful and decadent marble building on Corso Vercelli 40, in Milan's professional quarter, and she soon left the agency. She also accused them of improper collaboration.

The Riccardo Gay agency has long since moved, and is practically no longer in business, as its founder Riccardo Gay is said to be officially retired from business, Italian journalists have informed us. He is still, however, considered one of the best fashion scouts in the business. In the spring of 1995 he discovered a thirteen-year old Brazilian beauty Gianne Albertoni Vicente, who went on to become one of the most sought out fashion models in the world.

Bernarda Popelar, the most successful model to ever hail from Maribor, Slovenia's second largest city, and who is today a successful business woman married to a former state secretary for higher education Dušan Lesjak, mostly worked in Zagreb, Beograd and Milan. She could make between 500 to 1000 German Marks per fashion show with the Riccardo Gay agency, and up to 7000 German marks for various photo shoots. Because Popelar is nine years older than Melanija, the two never crossed paths in Milan. But many girls, among them probably also Melanija Knavs, have dreams that differ somewhat from reality and as soon as they get the feeling that things are not working out, and they no longer believe the agency will help them launch a successful career, they leave. The whole situation is made even worse if rumors start spreading about them through the fashion world, and soon everyone starts sidestepping and politely dismissing them.

But the fashion shows or catwalks that Melanija Knavs specialized in after her disappointment with photo sessions are, according to numerous fashion agents, even bigger time bombs. Everything there needs to be perfect down to the millimeter and second, and if anything goes wrong, then everything goes wrong. Everyone is always extremely nervous and stressed. This tension and the other bad sides to fashion shows are practically invisible to casual observers, but fashion critics, gurus, hyenas, and journalists spot them immediately, and have the power to destroy designers or models in an instant. They can destroy you much faster than they can make you. These days, says the fashion agent from Milan, everything is even more hyped, as the internet and social media have their own say, as well.

Melanija Knavs was in some ways ideal for the catwalk. Her height and other measurements were perfect, she was undemanding, unproblematic, *"wasn't a pain in the ass,"* and she always showed up well-groomed and well-rested. It was clear that she took immaculate care of herself and never indulged in any excesses like abusing alcohol or drugs, as her fellow model and friend Edit Molnar observed later in New York.

Melanija Knavs had perfected her walk, quickly memorized the choreography for any particular show, and had everything perfectly studied and figured out. The body she has today, though, has not been fit for high fashion for quite some time, as her plastic surgery and botox are too obvious, and have taken their toll.

The anonymous Milan agent also agreed that Melanija was perfect at the work that she did, and well paid, but far from the echelon of supermodels. The fact that she has graced the covers of magazines considered media icons of the fashion world is not the fruit of her labors, but simply the result of her personal link to billionaire Donald Trump. In his words, this is a situation *"when money talks,"* or at least when your surname does.

And it's true, if one were to sketch a timeline of her deals, fashion shows, and numerous magazine covers, it becomes clear that her career received a huge boost after her relationship with Donald Trump was revealed – especially after 1998/1999. That was her modeling boom happened.

"We really can't compare Melanija Knavs and her success in the global fashion industry with any other girl, who reached to the front covers and huge earnings through hard work, a lot of sacrifice, and exceptional talent."

The high fashion industry is very cruel, as only those models are considered with whom agencies believe they can produce highest quality products. The rules of the game are well-known, as well as the requirements, and there are no exceptions or room for maneuvering. Professionalism, time, and loyalty count, but success is only measured by profit. Million-dollar contracts separate the models from the supermodels, which are brands in themselves. Today the world's best paid supermodel is the Brazilian Gisele Caroline Bündchen, who earned $44 million last year and thus became the third highest paid woman in show business, right after the actress Jennifer Lawrence and the TV star Oprah Winfrey.

The first official supermodel was the legendary Twiggy, in the 1960s. After her modeling career she was also a very successful author on fashion and fashion advice, and was for a few seasons one of the judges on the extremely well-watched TV show America's Next Top Model. She was also the one who launched the emaciated supermodel look, as the burst onto the scene when she was extremely skinny, even bony.

Similarly to Wolfgang Schwarz, our anonymous Milanese agent also confirms that Melanija Knavs made it to the cover of the prestigious Spanish *Harper's Bazaar* in April 1996 because of the rumors that she and Trump were together, although officially they only made later. This was also around the time that Melanija Knavs, who had been living with other models in a different part of Milan, in an apartment owned by Elite, the agency she joined after leaving Riccardo Gay, also began moving to New York, where she ended up staying for good. She is said to have ended her personal relationship with Gregor Erbežnik, the Slovenian businessman who occasionally traveled to visit her in Milan and Paris.

In terms of her time in Milan, the political background of the Riccardo Gay modeling agency ought also to be mentioned as it is intriguingly connected to the course of Melania's progress. Its owner, Riccardo Gay, who lives in Milan, was at the time closely connected to some of the most influential Italian politicians of the then ruling socialist party, the Partito Socialista Italiano, led by, the now deceased, Prime Minister Bettino Craxi and former Minister of Foreign Affairs Gianni De Michelis. Several of the models working for Riccardo Gay got close to Craxi and De Michelis. The long haired De Michelis in particular, who was famed for his love of the night life, wine, good food, and who played an important role in Slovenia's road to independence, had a thing for beautiful, long-legged models from the fashion runways and TV advertisements. Italian journalists claim that Riccardo Gay provided the beautiful girls for the parties of his political friends. Whether or not the Slovenian model Melania Knauss was among those sent to party with these powerful Italian politicians remains unknown.

Another Slovenian model who also worked in Milan with the Riccardo Gay agency, but who wishes to remain anonymous, said that it was all done very subtly. Prostitution and sex were never mentioned; these were simply parties at night to which selected wealthy men were invited. The parties were organized by the agency and the models chose for themselves whether they wished to attend or not. It was true, however, that their chances of getting a modeling gig increased if they agreed to attend these parties.

A man called William Nelson also had something to say regarding Slovenian models. He introduced himself on Melania Trump's Facebook profile as a former fashion agent, active in the 1990s. Among other things, he also wrote that *"Slovenian models were practically on sale, especially for wealthy foreigners, because they wanted to get out of Slovenia. The girls that were beauty pageant contestants had a double price."*

"I watched," William Nelson says, *"how agents from their native country brought a dozen or so and lined them up in front of me, asking whether I wanted them to get naked. If I were wealthy, I could have bought any of them. The girls wanted out of Slovenia, no matter the price."*

Chapter 8

NEW YORK, NEW YORK

The former model of Hungarian roots, Edit Molnar now lives in the center of Paris. Born in Budapest, Molnar is now fifty, owns the boutique Leetha on Rue Saint Honore 420, and has two children with her rather well-to-do husband David Wizman. She and Melanija Knavs, by then Melania Knauss, were good friends, perhaps better friends than is normal for the extremely competitive world of modeling. They met in New York while working for the Elite Model Management agency in mid 1995 and became friends despite their dramatically different characters. Melania was very disciplined and introverted, while Edit was quite a party girl.

Edit was introduced to Melania through Paolo Zampolli. At the time Molnar was dating Zampolli who was, among other things, a business partner of the fashion agency Metropolitan, and founder of the agency ID Models.

Paolo Zampolli was born in Milan in May 1970. After living in Paris for a while, he became a businessman in New York, and was even one of Donald Trump's business partners as head of international development for the Trump Organization. Zampolli, in New York where he still lives today dubbed the Italian Ambassador, who also worked for the

United Nations, and is heir of a rich Italian family, played an extremely important role in the life of Melanija Knavs. He was the Italian American, or American Italian, who personally introduced Melania to Donald Trump, changing her life and moving the completely unknown Knavs-Ulčnik family from the middle-of-nowhere Podunk town in communist Slovenia to the epicenter of the Big Apple, to the very summit of New York.

When she settled in New York in 1995/1996, Melania Knauss lived on 14th Street in downtown Manhattan, in the Zeckendorf Towers, also called One Irving Place or One Union Square East, as it stands on the eastern edge of Union Square Park, near Gramercy Park in the neighborhood of Flatiron, and Greenwich Village. The four-tower complex houses 630 apartments, and has a central courtyard with a park and an indoor pool. Edit Molnar still remembers *"those beautiful, brick New York buildings."* Although this was Melania Knauss' first rented apartment in the States, it was a quantum leap in social status from the socialist apartment buildings in her hometown of Sevnica, or even from her apartment in Ljubljana, and to push the image even further she for some reason lied to the media, telling them later that after getting her feet on the ground in the States she immediately moved to Park Avenue.

But that was just one of a series of small lies that, after gaining fame from her relationship with Trump, Melania sold to the American public.

Then, in 1995, after her move to United States of America, Melania Knauss posed nude, under the name Melania K., for the French men's magazine *Max*. The pictures were shot by the French photographer Alé de Basseville and published by *Max* magazine in January 1996.

While Edit Molnar lived with her "boyfriend" Zampolli, Melania Knauss shared her apartment with photographer Matthew Atanian.

Matthew loved sports and took pictures for *Sports Illustrated*, *Outside Magazine*, *Elle*, *Marie Claire*, *People*, *Time*, and *Newsweek*, and his clients also included AT&T, Motorola, Reebok, and Disney. Melania and he were just flatmates, and, as Molnar confirms, he never, ever tried to sleep with Melania. Atanian knew, after all, that Melania was only interested in wealthy men. As he told later on, she was a *"typical older model"*; she dated very rarely, and when she did, it was always a well-off guy. This can lead us to the assumption that her goal was landing a wealthy guy, something not that rare for a model trying to make it. In the apartment, each had their own bedroom, sharing a living room, kitchen, bathroom, and balcony. Melania and Atanian split the rent, whereas the rather wealthy Paolo Zampolli paid all the rent for the apartment he lived in with Edit.

Paolo Zampolli always had lots of money at his fingertips, although he did not know how to handle it well. Many people succeeded in getting their hands on his assets, as he is said to have been too naive and too clumsy in business, though he desperately wanted to establish himself in the glitzy fashion world. Charlotte Hays, journalist and author of *The Fortune Hunters*, called him a *"guru of models,"* something he must have been very pleased with, while Melania Knauss was *"his protégé."* He was only interested in top models and supermodels, and was a known charmer and seducer.

Young girls fawned over his cars, usually rentals, as well as over his elegant clothes and accessories, which tended primarily to be Gucci or Versace. He had some trouble with his weight. He was not fat, but was certainly stout. Behind him and around him was a cloud of strong cologne, which he literally poured on himself, and his thick, black hair could be seen gleaming from a mile away. With that appearance, status, and family money he sailed through international high society, and continues to do the same today.

Paolo Zampolli is better known in America, New York to be exact, than in his native Italy. His close connection to Donald Trump and his slightly mysterious role in Trump's connections to beautiful women, in particular to Melania Trump stirred quite an interest with Italian journalists after the release of the first edition of *Melania Trump: The Inside Story*. Before that they were quite unaware of Zampolli.

Melania Knauss and Edit Molnar did most of their work for Metropolitan, therefore for Paolo Zampolli. Edit traveled Europe and worked outside of New York a lot, while Melania worked mostly in the States, predominantly in New York and Los Angeles. At that point her work was mostly for advertisements and catalogs. Then, under the patronage of Paolo Zampolli and his agency ID Models Management, Melania Knauss was said to have earned up to $1500 a day. Apparently it was Zampolli who invited Melania to come to New York in 1996 and work for him, though he later also loaned her to Elite Model Management. In another version of events Melania came to the States through the famed fashion agent Marina Masowietsky, who supposedly arranged a shoot for Melania with Redham cosmetics. This version is also confirmed by Jure Zorčič.

Apparently Melania Knauss was extremely bothered at the time, even frustrated, that despite landing numerous jobs, that all these were done as an anonymous model, without her name ever being mentioned. That is why, as Atanian says, she was *"never a good fit."* Melania wanted to be someone, land editorials, center stories in fashion magazines, where editors would also mention her name. Atanian photographed quite a bit for Marie Claire at the time.

It wasn't until just before she officially met Donald Trump in 1998, that Melania made it big. She became the main model for Camel cigarettes, so an image of her holding a lit cigarette appeared on a gigantic billboard in Times Square in the center of New York. Once again, though she was right there, in the middle of the Big Apple, she was anonymous.

In their private lives, the two model friends were quite different from one another. Edit Molnar was a party animal who liked to go out to dances and dinners, which was certainly made possible by Paolo Zampolli's money, while Melania was much more disciplined. Melania was always asking Edit how it was physically possible to be a model if you didn't sleep and get your rest. Molnar would often sneak out to the nearest store in the middle of the night and buy herself a tub of ice cream, and then eat it all. Melania would ask in shock, *"Oh my God, how can you do this?"* After all, as Edit says, Melania looked after herself *"200 percent."* Everything was planned and scheduled, from swimming, yoga, breakfast, and showering, onto work, lunch, work, and finally home. She apparently never left anything to chance.

Although completely different, Melania and Edit still hung out together all the time and became great friends. They went shopping and swimming together, got lunch, and even cooked dinner themselves occasionally. Melania in particular was a fan of home-cooked meals, usually soup, salad, and some pasta. While she never starved herself, she definitely watched what she ate. Fast food, processed food, or chocolate she barely considered edible, and she drank next to no alcohol. Her favorite and most common drink was the calorie-free Coke Zero, while champagne or wine only came into consideration on special occasions, and just a single glass, two at most.

When Melania returned home at night to her rented American apartment, she had a special ritual. First she showered, then removed her makeup, generally looked after her skin and hair, ate something, and then locked herself up in her room. She lived, you could say, a rather dull and extremely ascetic lifestyle.

Matthew Atanian says these days that there is not much to say about Melania, *"A typical old-school model."* She dated rich men, talked about her family at home, and took care of herself and her body every night. Paolo Zampolli commented on this to an American journalist, saying that it was unbelievable that *"this is a girl with a giant Camel billboard on Times Square, and she spends her whole day sitting at home."*

Edit Molnar remembers these wild times in the American fashion scene of the 1990s as the best time of her life. *"There were endless parties, we were happy, in love, we had lots of friends all over the place, and I don't regret even a second of those years.*" She also said that Melania was *"truly gorgeous,"* which can be easily seen from a picture of her with Matthew Atanian, who posted the picture of his former roommate on his Facebook profile. Atanian, who took a lot of pictures for the women's magazine *Marie Claire*, remembers that Melania was never an editorial model, and never played the main role in commercial catalogs, a fact said to have frustrated her.

"Such beautiful cheeks, gorgeous lips, and those heavenly eyes. Melania's cheekbones were very welcome in the world of high fashion; yep, you had to have a skinny face with very pronounced cheekbones. She's different now. I'm not judging at all; everyone does what they want. But to me, she was prettier then. I think I took this picture," says Edit Molnar.

On one occasion Molnar noticed that Melania, at the time not yet with Donald Trump, was wearing a gorgeous camel-colored coat. She asked her where she had bought it, and Melania told her she had designed it herself and had it made. Edit wanted the coat badly and Melania sold it to her, later Edit gave it to her sister.

"It's too bad that Melania didn't continue as a fashion designer, as she really has a feeling for it," Edit Molnar says.

Edit Molnar remembers that Melania Knauss first saw Donald Trump three years before they were said to have officially met. This encounter was in SoHo, during dinner at the well-known French restaurant Balthazar. This meeting was brief, however, little more than a quick hello.

After Melania properly met Donald Trump through Paolo Zampolli, she took a long vacation and got breast implants. Unlike her Zagreb-based plastic surgeon Siniša Glumičić, Edit Molnar was of course invited to the wedding at Mar-a-Lago, but she could not make it, as she had just given birth. At the reception she was supposed to sit next to Zampolli, Melania's idea, as the two were and are still good friends. Edit and Melania, former friends and colleagues from New York, maintain contact across the Atlantic, in the form of birthday and Christmas greetings.

Chapter 9

A SCENT LIKE HEAVEN
ON EARTH

A few select Slovenian journalists who reported on fashion and other social events received a somewhat secretive invitation in September 1998.

"Would you like to come along with us on Tuesday to Paris to advert shoot for a product with a Slovenian model, very successful abroad and with foreign photographers?"

Seven such invitations were sent, and the recipients flew, just for one day, from Ljubljana to Paris with the organizer from the modeling agency Elite. The Cessna that took them to Paris was owned by Ljubljana's company Gio, the company formerly known as Smelt. They landed in Paris' smallest airport Le Bourget, where small passenger planes land, and then took a taxi downtown to the Lutetia Hotel on Boulevard Raspali 45.

The journalists were told that this was an advert for a less known tobacco company that needed to be very careful how it advertised its products. But the focus of the journalists day-trop was a meeting and interview, as the organizers told the press, with the 28-year-old Melania Knauss, a globally recognized model, who was said to have flown in to Paris from the States just for this event. The meeting and the press conference with Melania were scheduled in her hotel apartment, number 211.

The guests and the journalists who were flown to Paris were given strict rules about how much time they were to have with Melania, how many questions they could ask, and were especially warned against asking any unpleasant questions. They were then promised lunch at the hotel's restaurant, where nothing on the menu cost less than 120 francs. Though the Slovenian press called it a glamorous hotel, in reality the Lutetia is only a 4-star establishment. An informal chat with Melania was also planned during lunch.

Judging from what they printed after the event, the invited Slovenian journalists proved themselves to be absolutely ignorant, journalistically completely naive, or even just plain dumb. They bought – hook, line, and sinker – everything that Melania Knauss told them, including even that she had won first place at the first Slovenian Look of the Year competition in 1992, although the Slovenian journalists should have known that that simply was not true. That "little" lie about her victory in Portorož, which bears witness to certain traits of her personality and was even repeated a few times in American media.

She also told them that she was about to start shooting a movie with Mickey Rourke, to be directed by Craig Singer, with the film hitting the silver screen the following year.

"To me this means a new challenge, a step further," she commented when mentioning the feature-length film.

Some Slovenian media even reported about the film in the subtitles to articles from Paris, but Melania Knauss never shot this or any other movie with the famous Mickey Rourke. Her movie career, if one can call it that, consists exclusively of her minor appearances in the TV series *The Apprentice*, produced by and starring Donald Trump. These only started in 2004. The year before and the year after she made cameo appearances in two completely obscure TV movies, namely *Miss USA*, 2003, and *Fashion Week Diaries*, 2005.

Dušan Nograšek, a reporter for the newspaper *Nedeljski Dnevnik*, still today the best-selling Slovenian weekly, asked Melania questions in Paris as if he were reporting for his high-school newsletter, while she responded with well-studied PR acumen.

"Since we know next to nothing about you in Slovenia, would you trust us with some basic information, to start with?" asked Dušan Nograšek, when he got his chance.

Melania Knauss told him, among other things, that her permanent address in New York was on Park Avenue, and that, in the fashion world, *"the best of the best are on the other side of the pond."* She went further to explain that she had only flirted with modeling in Slovenia, and that because she went abroad very early and found success, she had no experience with Slovenian photographers.

Melania Knauss was still a Slovenian citizen at that point (she got her green card in 2001 and became a U.S. citizen five years later), but the obviously very carefully chosen Slovenian journalists were not even aware of this.

About the Slovenian language she said that for her it was *"like a song, like a fairytale."* This was the line used in the title of her story as it appeared in *Nedeljski Dnevnik*.

Melania Knauss used the opportunity to boast to the press. With a manipulative sense for PR she placed herself among the top 50 global modeling stars, though, she mentioned, she was now flirting more with the idea of movies. She still planned on working as a model and said that, *"in the future my life will continue to be tied to the world of fashion."*

Melania did not want to talk about how much she was earning as a global modeling star, but she did say her three best traits were *"honesty, precision, and professionalism."*

"I am quite satisfied with my life," she said, adding that, *"I wouldn't change anything about me or within me."*

The next period in her life, though, flipped those words completely upside down. Shortly after she met Donald Trump she had several plastic surgeries, beginning to noticeably alter her face and body.

Sebastijan Kopušar, a reporter for now defunct magazine *Mag*, was a little more critical than his colleague Nograšek, although it is true that Kopušar only published his article in *Mag* about meeting Melania Knauss in Paris in June of the following year. By then Melania was already officially dating Donald Trump, who had initiated divorce proceedings with Marla Maples. In Paris Kopušar was most annoyed by the photographer Partho Gosh, who forbid the Slovenian journalists from taking any pictures with Melania Knauss, and at the same time sniggered pityingly when he saw the Slovenian photographers' equipment. In the end he demanded that the journalists leave their cameras and accessories in the hallway outside the door to Melania's apartment to avoid even accidentally snapping a picture.

To Kopušar Melania seemed excessively self-controlled, but, *"tall, beautiful, graceful, with soft movements, a professional smile that crept under your skin, and huge blue eyes that attracted your gaze."* Her chat, though, with Slovenian journalists, the one and only such meeting in her career to date, was *"professionally boring, so extremely boring that even the maids cleaning three floors above and below the room were yawning."*

Melania said *"almost nothing"* of her life, and *"such a story could have been written at home, comfortably snuggled up in an armchair with a glass of red wine in my hand, without even needing to use my imagination,"* the reporter from *Mag* maintains.

Nonetheless, Kopušar admits that, *"even with your eyes closed you sucked in this woman's beauty and her fine movements, and every now and again microclimatic air fronts would waft over a hint of her scent, which was Heaven on Earth."*

The most tragicomic part of the visit was during lunch at the hotel's restaurant, where Melania Knauss entourage are said to have looked upon the journalists as *"the model's poor distant relatives, who had come to visit their family member in a gilded palace."* The whole time Melania sat there, with her *"aristocratic beauty, talking so politely and calmly that it hurt."*

Sebastijan Kopušar was tempted the whole time to throw a plate on the floor, or at least burp really loudly and then slap his belly contentedly.

He did also admit that he and Donald Trump had something in common: *"Trump, who is unashamedly rich and has everything he wants, sees his blood pressure rise in the presence of one of the most beautiful Slovenes, Melania Knauss. And who can blame him, my blood pressure rose, too..."*

The following story also confirms how Melania's life really is full of unusual coincidences; In February 2016, almost eighteen years after he met Melania for the first and last time, Sebastijan Kopušar traveled to Iowa as a special reporter for the newspaper *Delo* and for Pop TV, in order to cover the caucus that had Donald Trump leading in the polls. Kopušar, who is the US correspondent for *Delo*, is one of those journalists who, at the beginning of Donald Trump's campaign, greatly underestimated him, giving him zero chances of getting a Republican nomination, much less of winning the presidential election.

Soon after the Slovenian journalists who had been in Paris published their articles about Melania Knauss, the famous Slovenian model living abroad, a first-rate jet set bomb hit Slovenia; Melania Knauss was said to be dating the notorious American billionaire Donald Trump.

The media reported that Trump was head over heels in love with the Slovenian model, and that she had even moved into Trump's luxurious Manhattan apartment. Some reports had Melania Knauss coming from Austria, and some even said she was Slovakian. Mixing up Slovenia and Slovakia, which are not even neighboring countries, is a common mistake among second-rate press agencies, and occasionally even among "serious" ones.

At the time Trump was still in the middle of his divorce from his second wife Marla Maples, the film and television star, as well as the former Miss Hawaiian Tropic, and was playing around with several well-known beauties, including the New Zealand model Kylie Bax, according to many the sexiest of the girls who ever dated Trump. Even more mysterious is his alleged tryst with the East German ice queen and multiple medal-winning the figure-skater Katarina Witt. Trump charged that Witt made up the affair for a bit of self-promotion, while Witt maintained that she never even knew Trump personally.

Some rumors even alleged that Carla Bruni, then a supermodel and today wife of former French president Nicolas Sarkozy, was responsible for Trump's divorce from Maples. Trump is said to have fallen in love with Bruni, who denies it, claiming that Trump said that just to gain publicity. She told the media that she was *"too smart to be dating married men."*

Also interesting is the unusual unraveling of events around the memoirs of the by then already divorced former Mrs. Trump number two, Marla Mapels, in February 2002. Maples had written her autobiography with the title *All That Glitters Is Not Gold*, officially announced by American publishing house ReganBooks, part of the publishing group HarperCollins Publishers. This happened in January, but a month later, in February, a representative from ReganBooks announced unexpectedly that the author and the publishers had come to the consensus that they would not publish the book. The rumors are of course that Trump intervened to tie his former wife's tongue on the basis of their prenuptial agreement; others say that he paid a fair sum of money to prevent its publication. Maples, for her part, called Trump a great guy after their marriage, saying that sex with him had been the best of her life.

On the sex front, Melania Knauss also publicly complemented Donald Trump during a radio interview with Howard Stern. *"We have incredible sex at least once a day,"* to which Trump added, *"and sometimes even more,"* also complementing on how good Melania looks in thongs.

Donald Trump has actually had a series of strange interviews with Howard Stern. In 2004 for example he told him that he is not a big fan of anal sex and that he has never heard Melania pass wind. She has never farted in front of me, Trump commented sincerely. Howard was then also interested in Melania's bowel movements. *"Melania has never done that in front of me, perhaps she is saving it for our upcoming marriage,"* Trump said, adding that his first wife Ivana's bowel movements are more normal.

Another interesting note here; both Marla Maple and Melania Knauss, Trump's former and current better halves, clearly both felt the need to speak out about how good sex with the New York billionaire is at the same time, both in 2000.

Marla Maples and Donald Trump gave their only child together, a daughter, the name Tiffany, after the famous jewelers in New York, and Marla Maples supposedly only received $5 million from Trump in settlement after their divorce. This was by any comparison far, far less than his first wife Ivana got, although Trump has been known to brag about how, despite demanding $25 million, that Marla only got one million .

Melania Knauss and Donald Trump certainly met before they "officially" presented themselves at the opening of the renovated railway station in Manhattan, the opening of the new W hotel in New York, and at the grand opening of the behemoth vacation hub the Royal Atlantis on Dubai's Paradise Island.

The official story today is that Donald Trump and Melania Knauss met at the end of 1998 at a party during Fashion Week in New York, with Paolo Zampolli making the introductions.

Zampolli, one of Trump's business partners, for whom he sells luxury – and accordingly expensive – penthouse apartments on Park Avenue for sums ranging from $9 to $30 million, and whose customers are mostly rich Russians, likes to brag that he is the one who *"discovered Melania Knauss and brought her from Europe in 1996, and two years later introduced her to Trump at one of my parties at the Kit Kat Club."* And seven years later, in January 2005, he accompanied Melania to her wedding with Trump. They flew to Palm Beach in a private plane, and Zampolli later said that *"it was the wedding of the century. Melania was so beautiful, so gorgeous."*

Zampolli also secured his afterlife with this deed, *"In Italy we say that if you introduce two people who then get married, you will go straight to heaven."* Paolo Zampolli is otherwise also known for wearing designer shirts with his initials – PZ – embroidered on them, along with Donald Trump cuff links with the Trump logo on them.

Jure Zorčič, Melanija Knavs's former boyfriend in Ljubljana whom we met in the first chapter of this book, has a completely different theory about when and where Melania and Donald Trump met.

Zorčič says that it happened in New York, at a private party hosted by former New Jersey Jets center basketball player Jayson Williams, who also played with the now deceased legendary Yugoslavian basketball player Dražen Petrović. Williams was later sentenced to five years in prison, charged with reckless manslaughter in the accidental killing of a chauffeur hired to drive Williams and a charity basketball team to events. Williams served eighteen months of that sentence and was released from custody in April 2012.

Even Edit Molnar remembers that she and Melania Knauss saw Trump three years before Donald and Melania officially met, in 1995, at a dinner in the famed restaurant Balthazar in Soho. Apparently they merely looked at each other, said hello and that was all.

That fateful September night in 1998 when Donald Trump – officially – met Melania Knauss, he arrived at the Kit Kat Club accompanied by the blonde Norwegian Celina Mildefart. Celina is today a wealthy businesswoman working in cosmetics. She is also three years Melania's junior, and entered the club that night holding hands with Trump. Melania was together with Edit Molnar and Paolo Zampolli, who quickly introduced Melania to Trump as he walked past.

Donald Trump had a reputation as a known fan of busty blondes, and his exes – from Ivana and Marla to Kylie Bax and Celina Mildefart – all had a certain resemblance on this front. But Melania is said to have fascinated him instantly, as Zampolli later told American journalists. Melania was a little more reserved than fascinated, but she did label Trump as *"attractive"* after their first meeting.

Donald Trump asked Melania for her phone number, which she refused to give. She is even said to have complained of his nerve, asking for a phone number while on a date with another girl. *"No way I'd give him my number,"* Melania told her friend Edit Molnar. Melania had also heard that he was a known playboy, and wanted nothing to do with him though she did like *"the spark in his eyes."* This was why she suggested to Trump that he gave her HIS phone number. At the same time she wanted know whether the number he would give her would be his work number, which she was also ready to decline, but he surprised her by giving her ALL his numbers, home, work, cell phone, the number to Mar-a-Lago – in short all the numbers he had.

Edit Molnar told the authors of this book that Donald Trump almost certainly also got Melania's number, but that it was Zampolli who gave it to him. Melania later bragged that Donald Trump sent his date Celine Mildefart to the bathroom so he would be free to speak with her.

Melania took a few days to think about it and called him after returning from filming an advert in the Caribbean. He picked up and they had a long conversation. Melania later reported that she could *"feel his unbelievable energy"* and that she was *"completely intoxicated by his energy."* On their first date, at the New York restaurant Moomba, a Mecca of sorts in the 90s for American and foreign stars, they reportedly talked all night long. Today Melania says, *"I remember that night like it was two months ago."*

When Melanija Knavs' old friend Mirjana Jelančič saw a picture of Trump, she remarked on the physical similarity between Donald and Melanija's father. In Jelančič's opinion Melanija had found someone she felt safe with.

Seventeen years later, when Trump was already on the campaign circuit ahead of 2016 elections, he said for a special issue of *People* that he fell in love with Melania the very minute he saw her, *"She was terrific. I tried to get her number, and she wouldn't give it to me."*

At the time Donald was still officially married to Marla Maples, whom he divorced in 1999, though they were separated from 1997.

When they met, Melania Knauss was 28, and Donald Trump was 52. The first events they attended as an official couple were the unveiling of the renovated train station in Manhattan, the grand opening of the W hotel in New York and the opening of the grand holiday resort Royal Atlantis on Paradise Island in Dubai.

They were most visible at the opening of the renovated Grand Central Train Station in Manhattan, an event organized by Caroline Kennedy Schlossberg, daughter of the J F Kennedy and his wife Jackie and current American ambassador to Japan, appointed by president Barack Obama; Kennedy's appointment was applauded by the Japanese public.

Caroline Kennedy planned the event mostly in memory of her famous mother Jackie, who, before her death, had undertaken to renovate the old railway station. Among the eminent guests were even Secretary-General of the UN Kofi Annan, Bill Clinton, the singer Placido Domingo, actress Goldie Hawn, the late John F. Kennedy Jr. and his wife

Carolyn Besette Kennedy, supermodel Cindy Crawford, the late Michael Jackson, and many more. The new pair, Trump and Knauss, were first pictured there by a photographer for the German magazine *Bunte*, confirming the rumors that they were, in fact, dating.

After Melania Knauss and Donald Trump started dating, her modeling career really shot off. She graced the covers of all prestigious fashion and trendy magazines, literally one after the other – *Harper's Bazaar*, *Glamour*, *Vanity Fair*, *Elle*, *Vogue*. She began receiving endless compliments on the fashion scene. Famous designer Oscar de la Renta, who died in October 2014, paid her a pompous compliment in public, saying Melania was *"the power of femininity"*.

She also began appearing as a guest on several talk shows, as well as Trump's reality show *The Apprentice*. She was also invited to take part as a judge in various juries, and when producers invited Donald Trump on different talk and radio shows, they usually asked him to bring his beautiful companion along. Her most famous modeling gig, from the period after she met Donald Trump, is an ad for an American insurance company Aflac. It was shot in May 2005, a few months after their grand wedding, and she appears in it as a half woman, half duck that is the mascot of the Aflac insurance company, quacking loudly once she discovers she has the duck's webbed feet instead of her own.

Typical of Melania, her often edited official biography on the web never mentioned her first ever magazine cover for the Slovenian magazine *Jana* in 1992.

Some insiders, including Wolfgang Schwarz, hinted that Melania Knauss received some of her modeling offers simply due to the rumors that she and Trump were an item even before the official meeting that night at the Kit Kat. Even her cover on the Spanish *Bazaar* in April 1996 is said to have stemmed from these rumors. This cover is also, interestingly enough, left out of her official bio.

What is also unusual and suspicious is why Melania Knauss suddenly decided to invite the carefully selected group of Slovenian journalists to lunch in Paris, never having done anything similar before or since. Conspiracy theorists are convinced that this invitation was directly connected with the bombastic news that broke just a few days later, that she and Donald Trump were a couple.

Melania's biggest media fame came in January 2000, when, as Donald Trump's new girlfriend, she posed naked for the men's fashion and style magazine *GQ* on Trump's Boeing 727. If Trump wins the White House this fall, then these pictures will, historically speaking, make Melania Trump the first ever First Lady to have posed for a photographer in the nude.

These very nude *GQ* photographs also became the subject of a cruel pre-election clash between Donald Trump and another Republican nominee hopeful, Texan senator Ted Cruz. An anti-Trump advert appeared with a photograph of Melania Trump from *GQ* magazine with the caption *"This could be your future First Lady."* Trump immediately responded on Twitter, threatening Ted Cruz that he would reveal his wife's Heidi secrets. Ted Cruz denied having anything to do with the ad, and all that Trump proved with his threats was that he is a coward.

Even when the photographs of Melania Knauss first appeared in *GQ* magazine in the year 2000, the authors of the article prophetically wrote that *"the rumors that Trump will run for President could mean that Melania will someday become the First Lady."* And next to it, Melania's statement at the time, *"I think every single woman wants to become that."*

Two weeks after the showdown between Donald Trump and Ted Cruz regarding the photographs of Melania Trump in *GQ* magazine some sixteen years ago, the famous American photographer who shot them, Antoine Verglas, gave his statement to *Forbes* magazine. He said that the use of the photographs for the disrespectful anti-Trump ad is a copyright infringement, as well as intellectual property theft, and that it clearly shows the poor level of the election campaign. The photographs of Melania on Trump's private plane were inspired by Bond girls. Verglas wanted to awaken sensuality and charm with the story of a private plane, a briefcase full of jewelry and a gun, and he was extremely surprised by the ultimate result. He had known Melania previously, when they worked together for a Sports Illustrated shoot. Melania was reluctant to go completely nude during the shoot, and Donald Trump was not present. According to Verglas, the sexiest First Lady in the history of United States is Jackie Kennedy and Carla Bruni is the sexiest First Lady of France.

Chapter 10

SLOVENIA
MEETS TRUMP

Late in the afternoon on 29 July 2002 a black Boeing 727
with the name Trump in golden letters on both sides of the
body and huge red Ts on both either side of the tail landed
at Ljubljana Airport. The plane was on its way to New York
from London and had made a slight detour to touch down
in Slovenia for a few hours, the only such side trip so far
taken by the private plane of "Slovenia's son-in-law" Donald
Trump to the homeland of his then still future wife Melania
Knauss.

False reports in the media indicated that Donald
Trump's visit to Slovenia was to herald the beginning of
his construction deals in Europe. But it is certain that the
Trumps have so far not invested a single cent in Slovenia,
let alone a dollar. Unless, that is, the renovation of the old
family house of Viktor and Amalija Knavs in Sevnica, worth
a few tens of thousands of dollars is to be counted among
Trump's "big European construction deals," pompously
predicted by journalist and chronicler for the paper *Nedelo*
and later *Nedeljski Dnevnik* Aleksander Lucu..

Earlier that day in July 2002, when still in London, before the Trumps flew into Ljubljana Airport, they had been driven around in the Rolls-Royce of the owner of the famous London department store Harrods, the British-Arabian businessman Mohammed al Fayed, father of the deceased Dodi al Fayed, the last companion to Princess Diana. When they arrived in Slovenia they did not – not even for a second – stop by Melania's hometown Sevnica. Her mother and father Amalija and Viktor had to wait for them at the airport, as if at a diplomatic liaison of foreign dignitaries. Rumor has it that Trump only agreed to land at Ljubljana after Melania relayed to him a special request from her parents.

Nonetheless, journalists from the paper *Dnevnik* wrote, three days later, on 1 August, a completely erroneous report about the *"American Billionaire Donald Trump at a Family Gathering in Sevnica."*

The weather at Ljubljana Airport was cloudy with signs of rain and, since Trump's plane touched down around 8 p.m., it was still light outside.

The Boeing 727 was commanded by Trump's trusted pilot Mike Donovan, and the plane was worth around $50 million. The ridiculously luxurious interior, boasting seatbelts adorned in 24-karat gold, with a gilded bedroom and bathroom, had been shown off to the public two years previously, when Melania Knauss posed naked in the plane for the British magazine *GQ*, lying there with only a bearskin blanket to cover her.

Three passengers stepped out of the plane: Donald Trump, Melania Knauss, and Norma Foerderer, Trump's assistant for many, many years, who more or less organized all of Trump's life.

Norma Foerderer died on 12 September 2013, and Trump tweeted, *"I have just lost my beautiful & elegant long time executive assistant Norma Foerderer. She passed away yesterday – a truly magnificent woman."* Norma Foerderer was one of the few people outside of the Trump family who had unrestricted access to Trump's apartments and houses.

According to Aleksander Lucu, who, along with his girlfriend and photographer Alenka Žavbi, with the permission of Melania and her parents, of course, waited for Trump and Melania at the airport, Melania had called Norma Foerderer *"my American mother"*.

But what Lucu writes about Donald Trump must be taken with a heavy pinch of salt. Trump's public relations people probably paid the airfare and accommodations for Lucu and Žavbi when Amalija and Viktor Knavs first flew to New York and then Florida to take an American vacation, so that *Nedelo* (the Sunday issue of the newspaper *Delo*) could cover the vacation. Despite all this, after coming back to Slovenia Lucu did not even know how to write the name of Trump's estate in Palm Beach correctly, calling it Merlago instead of Mar-a-Lago. Had this been his only gaffe, we could probably have ignored it, but he even accompanied it with an explanation that, *"the vacation home is on a narrow strip of property bordered on one side by the sea – mer – and on the other side by a lake – lago."*

Since Trump's plane had had to land at the special protocol section of the airport, there were two dark Mercedes' waiting for the guests right at the entrance, one of which was owned by Melania's father, Viktor, the other, an S-Class Genscher, was rented.

According to Slovenian media the meeting was *"familiar and heartfelt,"* commenting that *"Amalija Knavs and Norma Foerderer embraced warmly,"* although some sources claimed differently. Melania acted very strangely and aloof, so apparently Trump had to, almost patronizingly, nudge her a little, as if to say, these are your parents here, act accordingly.

What is almost certainly not true is what certain "insider" and "better informed" journalists wrote after Trump's arrival, namely that Trump said to Amalija Knavs upon seeing her at the airport that it was now obvious to him where Melania got her beauty from. The reason we can discredit this is that Trump had already met both Melania's parents when they came to visit their daughter in the States in 2001. It is of course possible that Trump used that compliment in his trademark communicative American style back then, although at the time Amalija and Viktor Knavs did not speak a word of English.

Aleksander Lucu and Alenka Žavbi, whose stay in America was supposed to have been paid for by Trump's PR representatives, are said not only to have met Donald Trump, but also to have become his *"good acquaintances."* They described Amalija and Viktor as *"excellent Slovenians"* on their return from their first visit to the USA, whatever that is supposed to mean. According to Lucu, Trump showed Melania's parents *"tremendous respect"* and that he was excited about meeting them.

Amalija and Viktor were shown Trump's business empire, his properties, and his golf courses, and introduced them to the *"the most famous Americans"* (Lucu doesn't explicitly state who these were supposed to be, but he does mention an Elton John concert, who is of course not an American, as well as a handshake with former Secretary of State Henry Kissinger), taking them to *"world-class events."* Viktor Knavs is also said to have been the first and last person whom Donald Trump allowed to sit at the wheel of his favorite Lamborghini.

In Florida the Knavses found out that one of Trump's neighbors in Palm Beach is the Canadian-American businessman of Slovenian heritage Robert B. Tomsich, who had in 2000 been awarded the Republic of Slovenia's Golden Order of Freedom by the president Milan Kučan.

Though Viktor and Amalija received a royal reception, they did not spend their time in New York with their daughter Melania and future son-in-law Donald Trump in their golden triplex penthouse at the top of Trump Tower, but they were settled into the Trump International Hotel along Central Park, near the Christopher Columbus monument. Why the couple didn't want Amalija and Viktor to stay with them, despite the enormous amount of space they had, is yet another of the many mysteries shrouding Melanija Knavs.

Despite the fact that Lucu and Žavbi, according to their own assertions, had become such *"good acquaintances,"* neither they nor any other Slovenian journalist knew anything about the background of the preparations for the arrival of Melania Knauss and Donald Trump in Slovenia, more specifically to Lake Bled. They were, however, apparently aware of their imminent arrival to Slovenia, as Lucu had informed the then Prime Minister of Slovenia Janez Drnovšek of their visit and even suggested he joined them for dinner in Bled. But Drnovšek refused the invitation, Lucu claimed in *Nedelo* this year, supposedly due to the *"expected stupid outbursts that would follow such a meeting in the media and with the opposition."* Lucu's statements can unfortunately not be verified as Drnovšek passed away in 2007.

By the time the two Mercedes arrived at Bled, that *"vision of heaven,"* as described by the Slovenian national poet France Prešeren, it was already dark outside. The trip lasted a good half hour, even though Bled is only about 20 miles or so from the airport. The cars stopped at the entrance of the Grand Hotel Toplice, still today part of the Sava business group that is indirectly still state-owned. For most of the duration of the ride Viktor Knavs was on the phone with Dušan Furar, head of facilities, who stood waiting for his guests to arrive.

The VIP entourage did not, however, enter the gourmet restaurant Julijana through the main entrance of the Grand Hotel Toplice, but sneaked in through the side door at the bottom of the thirty steps on the left side of the building that lead down to the lake front, while the road and the main entrance are a whole story above the water level.

They thus managed to enter across the restaurant's terrace through a smaller side entrance. Julijana, which has room for thirty guests, was completely empty. Even if anyone had shown up, they would not have been able to enter without an invitation. Everything had been prepared for Donald Trump's arrival, as the billionaire was adamant that he did not want any overly curious Slovenians hovering around him during dinner. Apparently not even the hotel's owners and its CEO, Andrej Šprajc, knew of the guests' arrival. How was this even possible?

According to what we know, four days earlier, when Amalija and Viktor Knavs found out that Donald and Melania would be taking a detour on their trip from London to New York for a brief visit, Viktor called the chief of facilities at the Grand Hotel Toplice, the bearded hotelier Dušan Furar. He asked him whether he could keep a secret, and if he agreed to do so, Viktor would bring an extremely important guest to dinner at the hotel.

When Furar gave his word, they began planning the visit over the phone and by email. Furar kept his word and Donald Trump's visit remained at the level of desired discretion.

The hotel's director Andrej Šprajc later reproached Furar over hiding Trump's visit, demanding to know why he had not been informed. Furar merely replied that if he had not kept his word, Trump would not have come at all, repeating what Trump had told him about not wanting any nosy Slovenian people around. Our sources also claim that director Šprajc was unaware of many things going on at the hotel at the time.

The guests sat around an oval table, turned toward the tall glass windows, with a majestic view of Lake Bled. Trump sat on the left, Melania on the right, and they both stared out over the lake during dinner. Across from them sat Melania's parents and Norma Foerderer, with their back to the window. Alenka Žavbi was not invited to dine with them, and, as Lucu was no longer with them at this point, waited in the restaurant's foyer instead.

At Viktor Knavs' orders, Dušan Furar adorned the table with a bouquet of 35 red roses as a reminder that on the same day, 29 July, 35 years earlier he and Amalija got married at the City Hall in Ljubljana. A bouquet similar to the one Furar had placed on the table had also been brought by the guests to mark the occasion. During this small celebration Donald Trump patted Viktor Knavs on the shoulder and warmly kissed Amalija on both cheeks. Melania was supposedly touched by the gestures.

Before dinner they treated themselves to a magnificent view of Bled Lake at night, lucky to have avoided the rain, a fairly common summer phenomenon in the picturesque Alpine valley where the lake is located.

No alcohol at all was served at dinner, not even a glass of champagne or an aperitif. The guests were served a pure fruit cocktail upon arrival, then Trump ordered a Coke Zero, and the others had freshly-squeezed orange juice. Not even the chef knew who he was cooking for, just what Dušan Furar told him, that they were very important guests. To start off, Furar – who by Viktor Knavs's order was the only server – gave everyone a soup or salad. Melania nibbled at this salad most of the evening, and Trump enjoyed an onion escalope with sautéed potatoes, which he complimented on. For dessert Trump devoured a dish of fresh forest blueberries, hand-picked from the nearby mountainous plateau Pokljuka, but without cream or sugar. He also turned down coffee. During dinner, which lasted around two hours, Melania acted as translator.

After dinner, as they were leaving through the back door and climbing the steps back up to the street level, Trump looked at Lake Bled one more time, and enthusiastically asked Viktor whether the Grand Hotel Toplice was for sale. In the hotel bar next to the reception they had a group photograph taken. The photographer was Alenka Žavbi, who also took a picture just of Melania and Donald; that picture is on display at the hotel today in a glass frame, along with the pictures of many other famous guests to the Grand Hotel Toplice, from the former Yugoslavian president and dictator Josip Broz Tito, to Michael Moore, Andy McDowell, Laura Bush, and Madeline Albright, and even the heir to the British throne, Prince Charles. The only thing wrong is the date added to the photograph of Trump and Melania. Instead of 2002, it says 2004.

Donald Trump was driven directly back to the airport from Bled, as he and Norma Foerderer immediately flew back to New York, while Melania spent a few more days with her parents in Sevnica. Her sister Ines was not at Ljubljana Airport to welcome her, and was not present at that family dinner in Bled either. Nobody knows why.

Today Donald Trump has upgraded his airplanes, also for the purposes of his presidential campaign, flying a dark-blue Boeing 757, which he bought in 2011 from Paul Allen, co-founder of Microsoft, for $100 million. His fleet also includes a Cessna Citation X, and three Sikorsky helicopters.

In addition to the money, small change really, that Donald Trump put into renovating the Knavs family house in

Sevnica, journalists in Ljubljana were convinced for a time that Trump was set to buy one of the planned penthouses with a pool at the top of the new, elite apartment complex Šumi in Ljubljana, which the well-known Slovenian transitional financial tycoons Matjaž Gantar and Sergej Racman of the financial holding KD Group were planning to build. Each was to cost around a million and a half euros. But nothing ever came of this ambitious construction project, and the never-to-be Šumi complex is now just a large temporary parking lot in the middle of Ljubljana.

Meanwhile, just this year, the sale of the Grand Hotel Toplice at Bled, or the entire, extremely indebted Sava Group, was the subject of brutal political and entrepreneurial altercations within the Slovenian transitional elite.

Igor Bavčar, a former influential Slovenian politician, was also interested in Donald Trump when he was the CEO of the petroleum company Istrabenz in the Slovenian coastal and port town of Koper. He called Viktor Knavs a number of times, at least that's what Viktor boasted about to parliament member Matjaž Han, to see if Trump would be interested in taking over one of the most magnificent hotels on the Slovenian Coast, the old Hotel Palace in the heart of Portorož. When Trump told Bavčar via Knavs that he would be happy to lend his name and the Trump brand to the hotel in Portorož, as long as Istrabenz paid for it, Bavčar never got in touch again.

As far as the relationship between Viktor Knavs and the Member of Parliament Matjaž Han, there is also the interesting detail that Han brought to Knavs the former Slovenian Prime Minister and current President Borut Pahor. At that point Pahor was only the president of his political party, the Social Democrats, but he was a fan of classic cars and wanted to buy an old Mercedes. He and Han visited Viktor Knavs, but Pahor decided against buying his car.

Recently Melania Trump's parents have been partly living in the States, spending half the year in New York or Palm Beach. In New York they stay at Trump Tower, and they spend the rest of the year in Sevnica. A few months ago they also went to Radeče, to attend the funeral of Matjaž Han's mother. Viktor Knavs also has an apartment in Nova Gorica on the Italian border, which he bought many years ago, supposedly with the money he got from his Ljubljana-based company Knaus-Haus. When the Knavses visit Slovenia, Viktor likes to boast around the local bars in Sevnica, that when he lives in New York he has servants attending to him all day and he can get them to serve him whatever his heart desires, but that he does miss Slovenian home made soup.

Melania's sister Ines Knavs, on the other hand, lives in America permanently, working for Trump, currently in fact on his campaign trail. She often posts fashion design sketches from the time she studied in Ljubljana on her Facebook page.

The meal at Grand Hotel Toplice in Bled was to date Trump's only trip to Slovenia, but in March 2005, a good two months after he and Melania got married in Florida, he paid a visit to attorney Bernard R. Diamond, head of his legal team, who represented Trump during his financially very difficult divorce from Ivana. Diamond sent a letter to the daily tabloid *Slovenske Novice*, still today the most widely-sold Slovenian newspaper, introducing himself as executive vice-president and general advisor to The Trump Organization. The letter came in a FedEx Express enveloped sloppily taped together like something Tom Hanks would have fashioned in his 1999 blockbuster *Cast Away*, and the address clearly showed it had been sent directly from 725 Fifth Avenue in New York, the address of the famous Trump Tower and the Trumps' official residence.

The letter, a response to an article written by Bojan Požar, one of the authors of this book, at the time still a journalist at *Slovenske Novice* and an editor of its weekly supplement *Bulvar*, was full of mistakes (in the letter Diamond carelessly misspelled the name of the then editor-in-chief of *Slovenske Novice* Marjan Bauer, writing *Marfan* instead), but the gist of it was as follows: *Referring to the article published 2 March 2005 I would like to point out the following: The claims made about Mrs. Trump could not have been true at the time your article was published, as Mrs. Trump has never heard of or met Petar Radović. As there is no basis for Petar Radović' comments with regards to Mrs. Trump, it appears that certain elements of the story must be completely imagined. Besides, Mrs. Trump is depicted in a very negative way, supposedly to attract your readership. This is a clear case of her reputation being tarnished, damaging her potential professional entrepreneurial options in the future. Such reporting ignores all the accepted standards of honest and diligent journalism and cannot be accepted.* The letter demanded a retraction and an apology in the next issue, or else the Trumps would exhaust all legal options at their disposal.

In consultation with the paper's editors and the legal affairs department of the newspaper *Delo*, the organization that publishes *Slovenske Novice*, Marjan Bauer and Bojan Požar decided that *Slovenske Novice* would not be apologizing to Melania Trump. This decision was made in the belief that the article in question, *Just Shoot Me!* (Požar borrowed the title from the popular – even in Slovenia – American sitcom) had not contained false information or shown Melania in a bad light.

Petar Radović's statement for *Slovenske Novice* that he *"had the feeling that recently Melania Trump's breasts look bigger"* has been proven, so it was impossible to believe that the article could have, as claimed by Diamond, *"damaged any professional opportunities Mrs. Trump might have had."*

"It is true that Donald Trump has almost gone bankrupt twice," wrote Požar, *"but if he does so a third time, it certainly won't be because of something written in Slovenske Novice, which sadly doesn't have the influence or the readership of the Wall Street Journal. We are, however, honored that Bulvar and Slovenske Novice are even read in Slovenian in Manhattan."* At the time, *Slovenske Novice* did not even have a website.

"CNN has also yet to report that Trump has lost some sort of billion-dollar real estate deal because of our article in Bulvar. As for Mrs. Trump's professional career and opportunities, we are certain that by marrying an American billionaire she has already achieved more than she even dreamed as a beautiful young girl in Sevnica."

Bauer and Požar did not find Bernard Diamond's absurd statements about publishing the story without authorization and demands for a retraction even worth commenting on. Instead they recommended that Diamond learn how to properly spell the name of the Slovenian capital, which is not *"Jujbljana,"* as Diamond wrote, but Ljubljana. If nothing else, Melania Trump, who lived in the capital several years, should at least know that much. It is unthinkable that Donald Trump's first wife Ivana would have misspelled the Czech capital of Prague.

Instead of suing *Slovenske Novice*, the authors warmly suggested that Melania Trump should rather bring a suit against those in the press who, when covering her wedding all those years ago, had "unauthorizedly" written that Melania was from Austria or Slovakia.

The most interesting thing is how Bernard R. Diamond bizarrely claimed that Melania Trump had never heard of Petar Radović.

This is of course pure faking ignorance, as Radović was the director of the live broadcast of the first Slovenian Look of the Year competition in Portorož in 1992, which was an enormous and integral stepping stone in the career of Melanija Knavs.

Marjan Bauer and Bojan Požar did allow for the possibility that the newlywed Mrs. Trump perhaps cannot – or doesn't want to – remember everything that happened to her thirteen years earlier when she was an aspiring beauty from Sevnica. Perhaps this useful selective amnesia was also setting the scene for the possibility of her husband once mounting a serious bid for the White House.

Despite the fact that the request for an apology was rejected, Melania and Donald Trump did not file suit against

Slovenske Novice or Bojan Požar, nor did the attorney Bernard R. Diamond do so in their name.

Donald Trump is otherwise known for his many lawsuits, including many against journalists and publicists. His biggest to date was against Timothy L. O'Brien, journalist and author of *Trump Nation: The Art of Being The Donald Trump*, published in 2005. Trump filed suit against O'Brien because O'Brien had written in his book that Trump's assets were worth $150 million to $250 million, making Trump a millionaire instead of a billionaire. O'Brien had cited three anonymous sources. Donald Trump sued him for libel and defamation and demanded extraordinary compensation to the tune of $5 billion. But he lost the suit. First in 2009 at the lower court in New Jersey, which threw the case out, and then the rejection was confirmed in 2011 by a New Jersey appeals court.

Chapter 11

JUST THE WAY YOU ARE

Melania Knauss and Donald Trump had their first and to date worst personal crisis in 1999, when Trump first started campaigning to become US President, as Clinton was wrapping up his second term. Trump, 53 years old and one of America's favorite tycoons, said in a conversation with Larry King Live on CNN, an extremely popular late night show run by an even more popular host, that he was assembling a campaign team to assess whether or not his candidacy would make sense. If they decided that it would, he would officially announce his campaign the following year, in January of 2000.

Trump bragged that as a presidential candidate he would offer voters a sound and productive economic and political program, that he would fund his campaign mostly himself, and that his first choice for vice-president was Oprah Winfrey, to date the highest-paid television host in history.

Slovenian journalists had barely recovered from the news of Melania was dating Donald Trump (though some like Petra Kancler, a Slovenian tabloidist who was invited to Mar-a-Lago to cover an authorized story for the magazine

Obrazi, were still writing her name in its Slovenian form, Melanija Knavs, rather than Melania Knauss that had been her official name for a few years), when they had to come up with new extravagant headlines like, *"Will the First Lady be a Slovenian?"* or *"Naked Slovenian to Be First Lady?"*

After Melania started dating Trump, her lifestyle changed under his guidance. She turned from a bit of a homebody into a true party girl, a fact first noticed by her friend Edit Molnar. Before she was shy and reserved, now she was going out and shopping at the best boutiques and shops in the world, apparently never returning to her own apartment without a new pair of shoes, mostly from the prestigious Manolo Blahnik. She kept her rented apartment downtown, but she was more or less living with Trump at Trump Tower.

When Donald Trump announced his presidential campaign in 1999, Melania Knauss was still working as a model. She told the New York Times that, as First Lady, she would be *"very traditional, like Betty Ford or Jackie Kennedy,"* and that she would *"support Donald."* But American journalists and part of the public, as Charlotte Hays describes in *The Fortune Hunters*, would have had a hard time imagining that Betty and Gerald Ford or Jackie and John F. Kennedy would sit down for the type of interview that Melania and Donald Trump indulged in with America's most (in)famous radio host, Howard Stern. About sex and cellulite. They discussed the incredible sex they have at least once a day. During the interview Stern asked Melania if cellulite was a threat to her beauty, and Trump interjected, saying that Melania didn't even know what cellulite was, since Trump *"doesn't deal with cellulite"*.

There is a whole range of odd things Donald Trump discussed in his interviews with Howard Stern. In 2004, for instance, he said he wasn't a big fan of anal sex and that he had never heard Melania fart, volunteering the information without even being asked or prompted. Howard then asked what the situation was with *"doody."* Trump answered that, *"I've never seen any, it's amazing. Maybe they save that for after marriage."* He then added that his first wife Ivana's digestion was *"a little more normal."*

The New York Times responded to this radio interview with a picture of Melania and Donald lying in bed, with a dollar sign covering Trump's head. Melania responded to the caricature, saying that sometimes the press *"could be very mean,"* and that she wasn't with Donald Trump for the money. *"I think you can't be with the person if it's not love, if they don't satisfy you. You can't hug a beautiful apartment. You can't hug a private airplane. You can't talk to them."*

Then, after a few months of romance, during which Donald called Melania *"his supermodel,"* they abruptly went their separate ways. Slovenian media speculated that this was a move on Trump's part, tied to his presidential campaign. According to the tabloid *The New York Post*, Trump broke off the relationship in January 2000, and Melania was devastated. The Post said that Trump had decided to do because he wanted to be alone for a little while, and that separating from Melania was *"the hardest thing Trump ever had to do."* Trump had told her he was breaking it off, sat on his plane and flew to Florida, while Melania cried herself to sleep in New York.

Donald Trump's friends were not really surprised, as their romance had started so soon after he and Marla Maples split up. He always talked about Marla Maples and Ivana Trump with the same passion, and he is said never to have stopped loving them. He also did not want to talk much about a wedding with Melania, saying it was *"too soon."* His friends pointed out that after separating from Marla Maples he didn't really need a new romantic relationship, but a friend and companion. And Melania had been just that, and had done well, but at the same time she had *"a total monopoly on his spare time."* Many of his friends thought, accordingly, that he would never go back to her.

Although Trump maintained that he had left Melania, there are some, mostly her friends, who say that it was Melania who broke up with him, not the other way around. Reporters from the *New York Post* said that Melania caught Donald fooling around with a Victoria's Secret model, having found a towel in his apartment that had makeup all over it. The show National Enquirer's Uncovered ran a story saying that well-known tabloid reporter A. J. Benz, who was linked with the model in question, accused Donald Trump of having *"stolen his girlfriend."*

As far as timing goes, their breakup paradoxically coincided with the famous *GQ* photos of the naked Melania in Trump's Boeing 727.

Friends and acquaintances maintain, however, that both of them played their part in getting back together. Trump, who, as he wrote in his 2007 book co-authored with millionaire Bill Zanker *Think Big*, goes into every negotiation to win it, was responsible for putting the cards on the table, while Melania *"sealed the deal"*.

This is more or less the same thing that Tina Brown from the Washington Post later wrote:

Underneath all her fabulousness and gloss, Melania Knauss' staying power in his life is based on a shrewd understanding of her quasi-commercial role. One feels she will not make Ivana's mistake of competing with the Trump brand. But she also knows, as second wife Marla Maples did not, the difference between being mere arm candy and high-definition product enhancement. As one of her friends put it, *"For Melania it's never, Ask what the Donald can do for you. It's, Ask what you can do for the Donald."* Furthermore the Trump business empire was also looking after Melania's modeling career at the time.

On the other hand, American model Chrissy Teigen, wife of musician John Legend from Ohio, was a bit more direct about the relationship between Melania Knauss and Donald Trump, tweeting in 2015 [sic]: *"ok trumpers let's get one thing straight, we both married well and pose half naked, I'm not alone in this."* Donald Trump attacked immediately, retweeting a message from one of his supporters: *"Wow! Trashy gutter mouth woman. You can't hold a candle2 @MelaniaTrump when it comes2 beauty and eloquence."* Trump added that she, Teigen, wasn't nearly as elegant as his wife. But Chrissy's final tweet was interesting in and of itself: *"LOL poor Melania doesn't need to be dragged into this. She goes through enough already."* She did not, however, elaborate on what exactly Melania goes through.

The second bumpy patch in Melania and Trump's relationship came in 2011, six years after the wedding of the century in Florida. The media reported that there was another woman, a porn star named Stormy Daniels, who was exactly Donald's type; blonde and busty. The third crisis came another three years later when, once more, there was supposedly another woman involved with Donald. In Sevnica the rumors were that Melania was set for a quick divorce and would return back to her homeland. Viktor and Amalija Knavs, who as a rule do not comment on anything related to their daughter and son-in-law, as their silence was part of the prenuptial agreement between Melania and Donald Trump, responded to such rumors merely with the following words, *"A lot of things are said."*

For her part, just a few hours after the rumors erupted on Twitter, Melania posted a picture on Twitter of her and Donald playing golf in Scotland, where he owns a property. There is no real information regarding Melania having ever cheated on Donald Trump, apart from the cynical smiles of Peter Butoln, who supposedly got his information form Ines Knavs. But it is the most common question that American journalists have been asking Bojan Požar in recent months.

After six years of dating Donald Trump officially asked Melania for her hand in marriage. Melania of course said yes. Paolo Zampolli, one of those who had an insider's view on everything, told Charlotte Hays' publicist, that *"Melania had been completely loyal"* to Trump for six years, and so *"Trump was doing the right thing."*

Upon hearing over the phone Slovenian journalists' questions regarding the latest rumors, Viktor Knavs reacted nervously, even stupidly. *"Where did you get this confidential information?"* he asked the journalist Alojz Petrovčič of *Story* magazine, inadvertently confirming the rumors.

"I don't give statements on the family life of the Knavses, as I think that is a completely private matter; every individual has their own life. If I don't ask you about your children and they don't interest me, why do you need to know what's going on with my daughter Melania? I will neither confirm nor deny a thing!" Viktor Knavs was agitated and began theorizing for *Story* magazine. It seems here that Viktor forgot, or maybe never knew, that Donald Trump, along with his many women, was literally the hero of the (American) media, and not just of tabloids.

While Donald Trump was divorcing Ivana, political prisoner and later South African President Nelson Mandela returned to Soweto, America and Russia were carving up a new German border, and Buster Douglas knocked out Mike Tyson, but Donald Trump got more exposure than all of them in the media.

Nevertheless, although during Trump's first presidential campaign in 1999 (this campaign, run on Ross Perot's Reform Party, almost set a record for its brevity, as Trump announced already in February 2000 that he was bowing out) Melania Knauss as potential First Lady was met with a lot of skepticism and shock, the media this time round is a lot kinder and more forgiving. At least some. Emily Green-house wrote an article in *Bloomberg* entitled *Vitamins and Caviar* where she noted that America had gone crazy over the *"decorous, gracious, glamorous wife and mother. A model for First Lady?"* On the other hand, the *New York Times* published that Melania's thick Slavic accent ten years after moving to America was something strong enough to *"render scrambled eggs caviar,"* whatever that is supposed to mean. To put differently, the journalists at the *New York Times* clearly do not think Melania has truly mastered the English language yet.

Despite the fact that Emily Greenhouse was not sarcastic about Melania Trump, she did in fact ask herself whether *"having the Trumps on Pennsylvania Avenue* [would] *return us to the era of a masculine man, who doesn't change diapers, and the feminine woman, preening, perfectly polished, ruling the home sphere."*

Greenhouse is, of course, aware that Melania's presence in the White House would certainly result in a few changes. She wrote that *"President Barack Obama and the first lady, Michelle Obama, have been a White House model of a new kind of gender equality,"* having met, *"after all, when Michelle was Barack's supervisor at a law firm."* Donald Trump and Melania Knauss on the other hand met at a nightclub.

David Patrick Columbia, founder of the online portal New York Social Diary, which specializes in entertainment, wrote *"She has a quiet, gracious manner, and she is remarkable because of her beauty. She's European, and I have a sense that she's like a lot of European women. They have that talent for standing back and letting him be up front."* Exactly how much direct experience the American tabloid writer David Patrick

Columbia has with European women is anyone's guess. What is certain is that we should not count him among the ranks of feminists or supporters of feminism.

Donald Trump's first wife Ivana, however, is categorically critical of Melania. At a New York party where a guest remarked that Ivana would make a great First Lady, the New York Daily News reported Ivana as responding with a laugh, *"Yes, but the problem is, what is he going to do with his third wife? She can't talk, she can't give a speech, she doesn't go to events, she doesn't (seem to) want to be involved."* After Trump's election campaign began to gain momentum, Ivana Trump publicly backtracked a little regarding her thoughts on Melania Trump's capabilities as a potential First Lady, but privately her opinions remain the same. Melania is not fit for the job.

In December 2003 Slovenian media forecast that the wedding between Melania and Donald Trump would take place within months, though actually did not happen until 22 January 2005. Before it could happen, Trump's lawyers had to draw up a prenuptial agreement for Melania.

As a good businessman, Donald Trump knew he had to have a prenuptial agreement. In his book *Think Big: Make It Happen in Business and Life*, Trump admitted that without prenuptial agreements between him and his first two wives he would have been left with nothing today, as, according to him, they were rather brutal in the divorce procedures. As a businessman he has seen many bad deals and many a bad marriage, along with endless litigation.

Trump writes in his book that no business deal can get as bitter as a fight between a man and a woman who used to love each other. He goes on to describe three such examples. First, the divorce of a friend of his, whom he describes as a business genius, an animal who tore people apart, but was an idiot when it came to women. He never had a prenuptial agreement, despite marrying, and divorcing, four times, paying around $50 million each time. He then lists the divorce of Paul McCartney of the Beatles from his model wife Heather Mills, who by the way also had a lover from Slovenia, the skiing instructor Miloš Pogačar, and thus came to the country many times. Lastly he cites Nick Lachey's divorce from American singer and actress Jessica Simpson.

Donald Trump is convinced that it is idiotic to marry without a prenuptial agreement, though he admits it is not exactly pleasant business. And when Trump decided to marry Melania, he is said to have told her that he loved her with all his heart, trusted her, and that their marriage was going to be great, but just in case things did not work out, she'd better sign on the dotted line. The amounts and other dirty secrets of the prenuptial agreement between Melania Knauss and Donald Trump are of course a heavily guarded secret.

Melania Knauss and Donald Trump married on 22 January 2005, the 4th Saturday in January, at the Episcopal Church of Bethesda-by-the-Sea in Palm Beach, Florida. At the time Melania was 34 years old, and Donald Trump was 58. Trump wanted the wedding to be spectacular, since "Melania is a spectacular girl."

And what a spectacular wedding it was. Invitations to the wedding were sent to around 350–500 people. Reporters from both tabloids and serious publications called it the wedding of the century and all of them made fervent predictions about the event. The media reported widely varying numbers, but around 1500 well-known people who expected an invitation did not get one. Donald Trump later remarked that he made a lot of enemies with the wedding, as he could not satisfy the wishes of all those who wanted to attend the wedding celebrations. A lot of the preparations for the big event, however, he left to his soon-to-be wife Melania.

In addition to Henry Kissinger, Elton John, Liza Minnelli, Prince Charles, Oprah Winfrey, Luciano Pavarotti, Muhammad Ali, Arnold Schwarzenegger who came with his wife Maria Shriver, the wedding was also attended by Prince Albert of Monaco, New York Senator Al D'Amato, the Governor of New York George Pataki, entertainers Lionel Richie, Sean Combs, Russell Simmons, and Billy Joel, famous movie stars Catherine Zeta-Jones, Michael Douglas, Bruce Willis, Clint Eastwood, television personalities Larry King, Katie Couric and David Letterman, radio host Howard Stern, model Heidi Klum, baseball star Derek Jeter, and basketball player Shaquille O'Neal. Not to mention, of course, the Clintons, who are today Trump's most dangerous political opponents in the battle for the White House.

Surely there have never before been so many famous faces at a billionaire's wedding, much less at the wedding of a Slovene, and everyone was invited to stay for three days in Mar-a-Lago, where, besides attending the ceremony, they could also relax by playing golf or tennis. The media commented that so many stars were shining there that the night was as bright as day, but that, despite their star status, guests were not allowed to bring any recording devices or cell phones to the wedding and reception.

The only guests from Slovenia were Amalija and Viktor Knavs, along with Melania's older sister Ines. On the central wedding table her parents placed a candle that had until then only been lit once before, at Melanija's christening in Raka pri Krškem. They brought it from Slovenia and lit it to bless the marriage of Melania and Donald Trump.

The American television network NBC, on which Donald Trump appeared with his popular reality show *The Apprentice*, offered the Trumps $25 million to broadcast their wedding, but Melania convinced Trump to turn down the offer, wanting a little more privacy.

NBC and Donald Trump are otherwise quite familiar with each other as hard bargainers. When NBC stopped airing *Friends* and started broadcasting *The Apprentice*, Trump demanded for the next three seasons the same royalties as the Friends stars had been getting, $2 each million per episode. NBC representatives said they thought an agreement could be reached, but Trump responded by saying, that they had not understood him. There were six stars in Friends, so he expected $12 million per episode. Trump's demands got the producers a little worried but a deal was eventually made, admittedly for much less money. At least that is how Trump brashly describes the negotiations in his book.

Last year the American TV network NBC decided to cut all business ties with Donald Trump, due to his harsh statements regarding illegal immigrants. They also stopped broadcasting the global Miss Universe beauty contest, whose license owner is Donald Trump. After this decision by NBC, Donald Trump purchased NBC's entire share in the Miss Universe organization, becoming the sole owner of the beauty contest for three days, before ultimately selling all the shares to the WME-IMG business network. Paula Shugart is now the president of the contest.

During the wedding and at the reception that followed there were as many as fourteen helicopters with cameramen and photographers circling the sky over Trump's estate in Palm Beach, but to no avail; the wedding celebrations festivities were practically hermetically sealed.

Well before the wedding, representatives from magazines, newspapers, and photo agencies were groveling at Trump's feet to be try and buy the right to photograph the wedding, offering hefty sums of money, but Trump turned them all away. He signed an exclusive agreement for marketing the pictures with Getty Images. In the end the media were served with an incredibly poor selection of pictures, and the proceeds everything Getty Images sold went into the newlyweds' account. *Vogue* immortalized the bride Melania Knauss on the cover of its next issue, and titled their article on the wedding *How to Marry a Billionaire*.

Immediately after the wedding, newspapers received a single black and white wedding photo, reserved only for printed newspapers, and even for that they only had a three-day window, until 25 January, to publish it.

Donald Trump and Melania Knauss' wedding was big business for some people. Preston Bailey was the event organizer, having planned the weddings of several Hollywood stars. Melania picked out three themes – white, gold, and diamonds. The leading Ljubljana newspaper *Dnevnik* called the wedding the *"Slovenian business deal of the century."*

The wedding is estimated to have cost around $5 million, with $500,000 being spent on flowers alone. However, many of the providers figured out, apparently without Trump's instigation, that it might be worth their while to work this event pro bono, or at least with massive discounts. It seemed to some journalists covering the wedding that everyone was competing with each other to offer the famous groom the most attractive discount. The famous French chef Jean-Georges Vongerichten, who has lent his name to one of the restaurants in Trump's New York skyscraper Trump International Circle, did not charge a dime, while he usually has a $10,000 starting price for any such an occasion. The menu included beef tenderloin in leek sauce, one of Donald Trump's favorite, shrimp, lobster, caviar, foie gras, and to top it all off a seven-tiered chiffon cake decorated with 3,000 white roses, weighing in at a whopping 200 lbs. Donald Trump neither drinks alcohol nor smokes.

Bookmakers also cleverly took advantage of Trump's American fame to take in bets. The well-known betting company BetWWTS, which due to strict American gambling legislation has its headquarters in Antigua, even put out odds on whether or not the marriage of Melania Knauss and Donald Trump would last longer than a year. The odds were stacked in favor of a lasting union; those betting against longevity would have earned 4 dollars for every dollar invested, while those who thought they would last made a 1 dollar profit for every 6 dollars bet.

At his wedding Donald Trump wore an Italian suit from Brioni (incidentally named after the Croatian archipelago Brijuni in the Adriatic Sea, where former Yugoslavian dictator Josip Broz Tito had his summer residence) with a white tie, but he did not want to do anything with his trademark old-fashioned hairstyle. Not even the famous stylist Tom Ford, who lobbied with Melania, was able to convince him. Melania is said to have told him that she loves Trump just the way he is, even if that means a completely ordinary hairdo. The very hairdo that the well-known Slovenian singer Rebeka Dremelj says that if she were Melania, she would give him a haircut immediately.

Another good business deal Trump made before the wedding was the purchase of a 13-karat diamond ring for Melania, which he bought from Graff Diamonds, the prestigious British firm founded by Laurence Graff and run by Francois Graff. The ring cost $3 million, but Graff offered it to him for $1.5, and Trump told the *New York Post* that he would have been an idiot to have turned down that kind of a discount. Graff is said to have offered the discount without any pressure from Trump.

Melania Knauss' wedding dress and of course the wedding gifts are also business stories in their own right. Melania understandably went to a lot of trouble, even enlisting the help of the then editor of *Vogue*, André Leon Talley, whose opinion in fashion circles was highly regarded. Editor Sally Singer also offered her advice. Melania said she wanted a more modern look, but in the end she and Talley decided on a princess look, namely a completely white, sleeveless satin dress, with a very long train. Fashion designer John Galliano of Dior sewed it for her; it cost $125,000.

Melania Trump's wedding dress goes down in history as one of the most expensive of all time. It is matched only by the $400,000 Givenchy dress that the reality star Kim Kardashian wore at her wedding with Kanye West, the Alexander McQueen dress for the same price that Kate Middleton, the Dutchess of Cambridge, wore when she got married to Prince William, the $115,000 dress from David and Elizabeth Emanuel, worn by Princess Diana at her wedding to Charles, and Catherine Zeta-Jones' wedding dress, which Christian Lacroix made for around $140,000.

Melania Knauss' wedding creation was worked on by 28 world-class Dior seamstresses who spent a total of 1,000 hours working with 90 yards of the finest silk, sewing in 1,500 precious stones and diamonds. During their inspection of the final product is said to have left the people who saw it at Dior in awe. The luxurious gown had a four-yard long train with even longer veil and was so heavy that the experts at Dior rushed to advise Melania to have a good meal before stepping in front of the altar or she might faint. In the end what they did was that Melania put on her dress just before going to the church, and was transported there in a small truck. Due to the weight and width of the dress she had to sit on a bench instead of a chair during the ceremony.

Melania's wedding dress was also the first wedding dress to make it to the cover of *Vogue*. Until then they had a policy against putting wedding dresses on the cover. Due to the exposure that the cover shot in *Vogue* gained them, the Trumps got a big discount from Dior, especially since the 14-page article inside described in detail how Melania and Dior worked together on the creation.

During the ceremony, the reception in the great hall at Mar-a-Lago, decked out in the style of French king Louis XIV and which was renovated for a reported $45 million, Melania wore blue lingerie from La Perla under her dress. After the first dance she changed into a lighter and more comfortable Vera Wang creation. The whole time she wore shoes from her favorite designer Manolo Blahnik.

Not everything used at the wedding was bought; the world-famous jeweler Fred Leighton merely loaned Melania the necklace she wore, which was watched the whole time by armed bodyguards.

As is American custom, the wedding gifts were purchased in advance from a wedding list. Melania registered with Tiffany&Co. and Bergdorf Goodman in New York. Some of the American journalists who are critical of Trump commented that she had done her job in getting rid of some of Trump's notorious kitsch.

One of the items on the list was a set of Tiffany silverware for 12 people, coming in at a whopping $18,000, with the cheapest part of the set – a single spoon – costing $150. There were napkin rings for $200 and a coffee pot and tea pot for $4,000 per piece. Guests could also opt to purchase a silver pitcher for water at only $2,250. For the bedroom they could choose to give Bergdorf Godman sheets for $1,200, while the cashmere bedspread looks like a steal by comparison, costing only $950.

To fulfill one other wedding custom, the bride needed to wear *something old, something new, something borrowed, and something blue*. As mentioned, the La Perla lingerie covered the blue, the borrowed was the necklace, the new was the dress and the fact that Melania had planned the wedding herself, and the old was a family heirloom string of rosary beads that she carried instead of a bouquet.

The maid of honor was Melania's sister Ines, while Trump's sons Donald Jr. and Eric, both from Trump's first marriage with Ivana, stood in as best men. Neither Ivana nor Marla Maples were among the guests, both citing schedule conflicts. Maples said after the wedding that she was not at all jealous about Melania, adding that in fact the opposite was true, and that she liked Melania a lot. Ivana was more reserved, merely – and perfunctorily – reporting through her PR agent that she too found Melania likeable and that she wished the newlyweds happiness.

Donald Trump also had to explain to the surprised American media why Melania did not have any bridesmaids besides Ines, saying that such customs were not upheld in Austria or Slovenia. He probably mentioned Austria because Melania Knauss has often, since she first arrived in the States – apparently on purpose – allowed the media to report that she was from Austria.

The former Slovenian ambassador to the United States, Dimitrij Rupel complained that this misrepresentation as an Austrian even brought on a diplomatic dilemma at the embassy in Washington. When Rupel, who served as an ambassador from 1997 to 2000, attended the traditional diplomatic Red Cross Ball in Palm Beach Florida he found himself in the same hall as Melania Knauss but never met her. His successor in the position of ambassador, Davorin Kračun from Maribor, branded Melania as the *"great ambassador of Slovenia."* However, it was not until May 2016, in an interview for newspaper *Dnevnik* based in Ljubljana, that he described how Melania attended an event in December of 2000, hosted by the Kračuns to honor Slovenia's independence day. He was not really able to articulate why he considered Melania to be this great Slovenian "ambassador." What is interesting regarding this event is that the Slovenian newspaper *Dnevnik* says it was held in New York's Plaza Hotel, but another Slovenian newspaper *Večer*, which also published a photo of Donald Trump and Melania Knauss posing with the Kračuns at the event, said it was held in the Plaza Hotel in Washington.

After this event, where the guests were abuzz, not because of Melania, but because she came to the party with Trump, Donald invited the Kračuns to his estate in Palm Beach, where they went a mere few weeks later, in January 2001. And that is where Melania, according to Davorin Kračun, highlighted the fact that she was in fact Slovenian and that he was the ambassador of her country. *"The rumors that she has forgotten her Slovenian roots were never true,"* says Kračun and adds that, *"Melania was always in regular contact with the Slovenian Embassy."* Every year after that for the following four years, the Kračuns also attended an event in the elite Florida hotel Breakers as Melania and Donald Trump's guests. Apparently it was Melania who added them to the guest list.

After the Kračuns left Washington and the United States, contacts with the Trumps also ceased. Of Trump, who at the time sent his private plane for the Kračuns and on which they were always *"interesting company,"* Kračun now says is a *"political showoff."* Ivana Trump, Donald's first wife was also on the plane once with the Kračuns and Melania. When the Kračuns were in Florida, they stayed with Trump's neighbor Robert J. Tomsich. The attendance at the formerly mentioned event cost $10,000 and was covered by Trump for the Kračuns. The money raised went to the underprivileged and poor in the West Palm Beach area. However, then Slovenia's highest diplomat Kračun and Donald Trump never really had any serious conversations. Their meetings were limited to meaningless handshakes and small talk about what was happening in Slovenia.

Trump's words about bridesmaids not being a tradition in Slovenia are also incorrect. Just as in America, bridesmaids in Slovenia are also normally the bride's best friends or close relatives. There are entire books and websites in Slovenia dedicated to offering advice on how to choose your bridesmaids and what their tasks should be. The real question is not one of customs, but of practice; why did Melania not have any other bridesmaids? Truth be told, the American media has never reported on any of Melania Knauss' close friends. Edit Molnar, Melania's only known friend from their modeling days, could not make it to the wedding because she had only just given birth.

Donald Trump is also said to have, for understandable reasons, declined having a bachelor party. The only thing that hit a snag in the planning of the wedding was Donald Trump's desire for a nine-minute firework display. He did not get his way, as the Palm Beach City Council rejected his request, letting him know that money could not, in fact, buy everything.

The ceremony in the chapel started a little after 7 p.m. The door at the back of the chapel opened and the melody by Handel and Bach began to play. The witnesses, Donald Jr., Eric, and Ivanka accompanied Donald to the altar. Meanwhile, a floor higher, Melania was still thinking about how to safely make it to the altar in her Dior dress, she had no practiced walking in it at all. A little while after, the magnificent *Ave Maria* began playing on the organ and Melania was already heading down the altar with her father Viktor by her side. She groaned slightly when she set off, as the wedding gown was extremely long and heavy.

Nonetheless, at the end of the wedding, a few hours after Billy Joel had serenaded the guests with his ballad *Just The Way You Are*, chef Jean-Georges Vongerichten told journalists that Melania, who looked after even the smallest details in planning the wedding, from choosing the 10 inch gold-lined china plates to selecting the New York opera singer Camellia Johnson to sing the opening aria at the reception, had *"succeeded,"* adding that *"the bride's taste is truly refined."*

Exactly eight months later, in October 2005, news broke that Melania and Donald Trump were expecting a baby. Paolo Zampolli had in fact already been telling close circles that Melania was pregnant. The Trumps did not give away the child's gender at the time.

Their son Barron William Trump was born on 20 March 2006 in New York. Barron speaks English and Slovenian and, if Donald has not seen Sevnica yet, his son has so far never actually even been to Slovenia.

AUTHORS

Bojan Požar is one of Slovenia's most prominent journalists. He is the owner and editor of the website Pozare-
port.si, a blog that uncovers what goes on behind the scenes
in Slovenia and whose readership includes a large portion
of the Slovenian mainstream media. He is also the host of a
weekly TV talk show with the same name on TV3, a television channel with a national reach. Požar published the 2002
best-selling book *Dangerous Liaisons of Naked Slovenia*.

Igor Omerza, Master of Economics, was an active member of the opposition to the former regime in the 1980's and
an active politician after that. As a former Member of Parliament and Deputy Mayor of Ljubljana, he is the author
of numerous scholarly articles on economics and politics.
He has dedicated the past few years to writing and publishing books. Thus far he has published ten books, with topics
focusing on recent Slovenian history and the secret police in
communist Slovenia.

8316979R00166

Printed in Germany
by Amazon Distribution
GmbH, Leipzig